THE YEAR OF THE
LOS ANGELES
KINGS

Library and Archives Canada Cataloguing in Publication

Podnieks, Andrew
The year of the Los Angeles Kings : celebrating the 2012 Stanley Cup champions / Andrew Podnieks.

"The official NHL Stanley Cup publication".
ISBN 978-0-7710-5110-4

1. Los Angeles Kings (Hockey team). 2. Stanley Cup (Hockey) (2012). I. National Hockey League II. Title.

GV848.L68P62 2012   796.962'640979494   C2012-904054-1

We acknowledge the financial support of the Government of Canada through the Canada Book Fund and that of the Government of Ontario through the Ontario Media Development Corporation's Ontario Book Initiative. We further acknowledge the support of the Canada Council for the Arts and the Ontario Arts Council for our publishing program.

Published simultaneously in the United States of America by Fenn/McClelland & Stewart, a division of Random House of Canada Limited Ltd., P.O. Box 1030, Plattsburgh, New York 12901

Library of Congress Control Number: 2001012345

Designed by First Image
Printed and bound in the United States of America

Fenn/McClelland & Stewart,
a division of Random House of Canada Limited
One Toronto Street
Suite 300
Toronto, Ontario
M5C 2V6
www.mcclelland.com

1   2   3   4   5   16   15   14   13   12

THE YEAR OF THE
LOS ANGELES
KINGS

OFFICIAL LICENSED PRODUCT

NHL

PRODUIT LICENCIE OFFICIEL

2012

STANLEY CUP

CHAMPIONS

LA

Celebrating the 2012 Stanley Cup Champions

Andrew Podnieks

FENN

M&S

CONTENTS

INTRODUCTION

Not since Montreal in 1993 has a team won the Stanley Cup after starting the season seemingly so far from it. At the Kings' training camp in September 2011, no hockey expert could have intelligently predicted a Los Angeles championship. But the playoffs are not held in September; they are held in the spring, after a tough, 82-game, regular-season. The Kings qualified for the playoffs only on the final weekend. Seeded eighth and set to play League-champion Vancouver, the Cup finalists from the previous year, things looked grim for the Kings.

But first things first. Los Angeles general manager Dean Lombardi built his team through an assiduous combination of draft choices, free-agent signings, and trades. Such a team is not built overnight, nor does it develop the team chemistry needed to win the Cup over the course of a few games.

The Kings, as they appear now, started to come together in 2003 when Dustin Brown was drafted to the team. This was a star player you could build a franchise around. But like any star, he needed time to develop, and he needed a strong supporting cast. In the coming years, the Kings drafted Anze Kopitar and Jonathan Quick in 2005 and Drew Doughty in 2008. These three, with Brown, formed the core elements that were required to win the Cup. As well as making wise draft selections, Lombardi also used free agency. In 2009, the Pittsburgh Penguins won the Cup, but Lombardi snagged a key piece of that team, defenceman Rob Scuderi.

In 2010, he signed Willie Mitchell, an important role player. And in 2011, Ethan Moreau and Simon Gagne also signed on. He acquired Mike Richards in a trade at draft time. The roster was starting to take shape, but during the 2011–12 regular season, Lombardi made two more critical moves. He traded with the Blue Jackets for a good friend of Richards, Jeff Carter, and he replaced coach Bryan Murray with Darryl Sutter.

When Sutter came on board on December 20, 2011, he recognized a team with far more potential than it had showed. It had size, speed, skill, and toughness. It had a great goalie, a star defenceman, and a top line that could compete against any in the league. Even still, the Kings took some time to adapt to Sutter's system, doing so while battling for a playoff spot in the competitive Western Conference.

By the time the Conference Quarterfinals against the Canucks began, the Kings were ready. They peaked at the right time, and literally every element a team needs to win fell into place. Good results beget optimism which creates confidence and momentum, and the Kings started with a win in Game 1 and never let up until they were holding the Cup, grinning from behind their grizzled beards that are the trademark of any Stanley Cup team in the 21st century.

The Kings got incredible goaltending from Jonathan Quick. Drew Doughty, who endured some criticism during the season for putative uninspired play, was Orr-like on the blue line. Brown, Kopitar, Richards, and Carter led the attack. The supporting cast played with exceptional ability and intensity, proving again how the Stanley Cup playoffs forces players to take their game to another level – or be sent packing early. Dustin Penner, Slava Voynov, Jordan Nolan, and every man on the roster was critical to the win; every night it was a new player who contributed a defining moment to the victory.

The team blocked shots and played aggressively; it had superb penalty killing and a killer instinct. The Kings scored the first goal almost every game, won every overtime game they played, were a record 10–0 in road games and played only 18 games, tied for the fewest in the modern era.

Given the team's relative youth, there is no reason to believe this team won't make it back to the big dance soon, and often. The Kings won the Cup for the first time since joining the league in 1967, and made it to the Final for only the second time, but they'll be back – and sooner rather than later.

The history of the Los Angeles Kings begins on February 9, 1966, the day the NHL awarded a franchise to Jack Kent Cooke, a U.S.–based Canadian entrepreneur who also owned teams in the NFL and NBA. The team represented the first stage in the NHL's cross-continent expansion, which continued over the next three decades.

The Kings were one of six new teams that started playing in the 1967–68 season as the League doubled in size, ending the Original Six era. The other franchises were awarded to Pittsburgh, Philadelphia, St. Louis, Minnesota, and Oakland.

Once Cooke decided on the Kings nickname, he chose purple and gold – the colour of royalty – for the team's uniforms. They played out of Long Beach Arena at the start of their first season while Cooke built his own arena, the Forum, in Inglewood, California. The Kings played their first regular-season NHL game on October 14, 1967, beating the Philadelphia Flyers, 4–2.

The first star of the team was goalie Rogatien Vachon, acquired from Montreal in 1972. He provided superb goaltending and gave the Kings a chance to win every night, something they lacked the first few years of their existence.

The next phase of their development occurred in the summer of 1975 when they acquired Marcel Dionne from Detroit. Small and compact, Dionne was a tremendous skater who could both pass and score with great ease. Midway through the 1978–79 season, he was put on a line with wingers Charlie Simmer and Dave Taylor. The three clicked immediately. Dubbed the "Triple Crown Line," this trio became one of the top scoring units in the League. Dionne played some 12 seasons with the Kings, winning the Art Ross Trophy in 1979–80 and becoming the second-highest scorer in NHL history, after Gordie Howe (he now sits fifth on the all-time list).

The modern history of the Kings began in 1987, when Bruce McNall bought the team from Jerry Buss. McNall talked a big game and backed it up with his actions. Just a year after acquiring the team, he brought Wayne Gretzky to L.A. in one of the biggest trades of all time.

Gretzky delivered, on the ice and off it. He brought Hollywood stars to the Fabulous Forum, as the arena was called, and he was everywhere in

L.A., promoting the Kings and the sport. Gretzky almost single-handedly took the Kings to the Cup Final in 1993 for the first and only time prior to the 2011–12 season. He created an excitement for the team that had previously been lacking.

It was during the Gretzky era that the next team superstar emerged. Luc Robitaille started to develop into a phenomenal presence on the left wing. Graced

One of the greatest goalies of all time, Terry Sawchuk played for the Kings in the team's early years.

with a strong stride and blistering shot, he augmented the offensive firepower that Gretzky brought to the team.

In 1999, the Kings moved into a glitzy new home in downtown L.A., the STAPLES Center. Despite the impressive characteristics of the state-of-the-art facility, the team sagged badly. The Kings missed the postseason six years in a row before earning a spot in the 2010 Playoffs, where they suffered a first-round exit.

Today, with a modern building and a solid organization, the Kings are poised to be a contender for many years to come. They have a core of young stars – Anze Kopitar, Mike Richards, Jonathan Quick, Dustin Brown – and they have a fan base that is getting as excited for the new Kings as they were for Gretzky's Kings some two decades prior.

The Forum was home to the Los Angeles Kings from 1967 until 1999. Designed by Charles Luckman, the $16 million circular building was modelled after the Roman Forum. Its capacity of 16,005 for hockey was well-known to any fan who read game summaries in the newspaper. But, given that this was L.A., the arena was as famous for its concerts as it was for sports. A who's who of legends performed there, including Elvis Presley, Led Zeppelin, and Michael Jackson.

Former owner Bruce McNall stands outside the Great Western Forum, often simply called the Fabulous Forum.

Compared to the Forum, the $375 million STAPLES Center is a veritable colossus. Nearly a million square feet, it seats 18,118 for hockey. It opened on October 17, 1999, with a Bruce Springsteen concert, and hosted the NHL All-Star Game in 2002 and the NHL Entry Draft in 2010. The arena also acts as home base for both the L.A. Lakers and L.A. Clippers of the National Basketball Association.

The STAPLES Center is the current home of the Kings and a state-of-the-art sports complex with few equals in North America.

The 2011–12 Season

Player	2011–12 Status
Justin Azevedo	Manchester, AHL
Andy Andreoff	Oshawa, OHL; Manchester, AHL
Jonathan Bernier	Los Angeles, NHL
Jean-Francois Berube	Ontario, ECHL
Dustin Brown	Los Angeles, NHL
Michal Cajkovski	Ottawa, OHL
Andrew Campbell	Manchester, AHL
Taylor Carnevale	Sarnia, OHL; Shawinigan, QMJHL
Marc-Andre Cliche	Manchester, AHL
Kyle Clifford	Los Angeles, NHL
Rich Clune	Manchester, AHL
Robert Czarnik	Manchester, AHL
Nicolas Deslauriers	Manchester, AHL
Drew Doughty	Los Angeles, NHL
Davis Drewiske	Los Angeles, NHL
Pierre Durepos	Saint John, QMJHL
Colin Fraser	Los Angeles, NHL
Simon Gagne	Los Angeles, NHL
Christopher Gibson	Chicoutimi, QMJHL
Matt Greene	Los Angeles, NHL
Shaun Heshka	Binghamton and Peoria, AHL
Thomas Hickey	Manchester, AHL
Trent Hunter	Los Angeles, NHL
Martin Jones	Manchester, AHL
Jack Johnson	traded to Columbus, NHL
Justin Johnson	Manchester, AHL
Michael Kantor	Sudbury and Sault Ste. Marie, OHL
Ray Kaunisto	Manchester, AHL
Dwight King	Manchester, AHL; Los Angeles, NHL
David Kolomatis	Manchester, AHL
Anze Kopitar	Los Angeles, NHL
Brandon Kozun	Manchester, AHL
Trevor Lewis	Los Angeles, NHL
Andrei Loktionov	Los Angeles, NHL
Ray Macias	Toronto and Springfield, AHL; Reading, ECHL
Alec Martinez	Los Angeles, NHL
David Meckler	Manchester, AHL
Rob Mignardi	Manchester and Houston, AHL
Colin Miller	Sault Ste. Marie, OHL
Willie Mitchell	Los Angeles, NHL
Ethan Moreau	Los Angeles, NHL
Michael Morrison	Peterborough, OHL
Patrick Mullen	Manchester, AHL
Jake Muzzin	Manchester, AHL
Jordan Nolan	Los Angeles, NHL
Cam Paddock	Manchester, AHL
Scott Parse	Los Angeles, NHL
Dustin Penner	Los Angeles, NHL
Jonathan Quick	Los Angeles, NHL
Mike Richards	Los Angeles, NHL
Brad Richardson	Los Angeles, NHL
Alex Roach	Calgary, WHL
Michael Schumacher	Sault Ste. Marie, OHL
Rob Scuderi	Los Angeles, NHL
Jarret Stoll	Los Angeles, NHL
C.J. Stretch	Houston, AHL; Ontario, ECHL
Tyler Toffoli	Ottawa, OHL
Linden Vey	Manchester, AHL
Slava Voynov	Los Angeles, NHL
J.D. Watt	Manchester, AHL; Ontario, ECHL
Jordan Weal	Regina, WHL
Kevin Westgarth	Los Angeles, NHL
Justin Williams	Los Angeles, NHL
Teigan Zahn	University of Calgary, CWUAA
Jeff Zatkoff	Manchester, AHL

EASTERN CONFERENCE

	GP	W	L	OT	GF	GA	Pts
NY Rangers	82	51	24	7	226	187	109
Boston	82	49	29	4	269	202	102
Florida	82	38	26	18	203	227	94
Pittsburgh	82	51	25	6	282	221	108
Philadelphia	82	47	26	9	264	232	103
New Jersey	82	48	28	6	228	209	102
Washington	82	42	32	8	222	230	92
Ottawa	82	41	31	10	249	240	92
Buffalo	82	39	32	11	218	230	89
Tampa Bay	82	38	36	8	235	281	84
Winnipeg	82	37	35	10	225	246	84
Carolina	82	33	33	16	213	243	82
Toronto	82	35	37	10	231	264	80
NY Islanders	82	34	37	11	203	255	79
Montreal	82	31	35	16	212	226	78

WESTERN CONFERENCE

	GP	W	L	OT	GF	GA	Pts
Vancouver	82	51	22	9	249	198	111
St. Louis	82	49	22	11	210	165	109
Phoenix	82	42	27	13	216	204	97
Nashville	82	48	26	8	237	210	104
Detroit	82	48	28	6	248	203	102
Chicago	82	45	26	11	248	238	101
San Jose	82	43	29	10	228	210	96
Los Angeles	82	40	27	15	194	179	95
Calgary	82	37	29	16	202	226	90
Dallas	82	42	35	5	211	222	89
Colorado	82	41	35	6	208	220	88
Minnesota	82	35	36	11	177	226	81
Anaheim	82	34	36	12	204	231	80
Edmonton	82	32	40	10	212	239	74
Columbus	82	29	46	7	202	262	65

L.A. KINGS 2011–12 REGULAR SEASON RECORD

October 7	NY Rangers 2 vs. Los Angeles 3 (Stockholm, Sweden) (OT)
October 8	Buffalo 4 vs. Los Angeles 2 (Berlin, Germany)
October 13	Los Angeles 1 at New Jersey 2 (SO)
October 15	Los Angeles 3 at Philadelphia 2 (OT)
October 18	St. Louis 0 at Los Angeles 5
October 20	Los Angeles 2 at Phoenix 0
October 22	Dallas 0 at Los Angeles 1
October 25	New Jersey 3 at Los Angeles 0
October 27	Los Angeles 5 at Dallas 3
October 29	Los Angeles 2 at Phoenix 3 (OT)
October 30	Los Angeles 2 at Colorado 3
November 3	Edmonton 3 at Los Angeles 0
November 5	Pittsburgh 3 at Los Angeles 2 (SO)
November 7	Los Angeles 2 at San Jose 4
November 8	Nashville 3 at Los Angeles 4
November 10	Vancouver 3 at Los Angeles 2
November 12	Minnesota 2 at Los Angeles 5
November 16	Anaheim 1 at Los Angeles 2 (SO)
November 17	Los Angeles 5 at Anaheim 3
November 19	Detroit 4 at Los Angeles 1
November 22	Los Angeles 3 at St. Louis 2
November 23	Los Angeles 2 at Dallas 3 (OT)
November 26	Chicago 2 at Los Angeles 1
November 28	San Jose 0 at Los Angeles 2
December 1	Florida 1 at Los Angeles 2
December 3	Montreal 2 at Los Angeles 1
December 6	Los Angeles 2 at Anaheim 3
December 8	Minnesota 4 at Los Angeles 2
December 10	Dallas 2 at Los Angeles 1
December 13	Los Angeles 0 at Boston 3
December 15	Los Angeles 2 at Columbus 1
December 17	Los Angeles 2 at Detroit 8
December 19	Los Angeles 3 at Toronto 2 (SO)
December 22	Anaheim 2 at Los Angeles 3 (SO)
December 23	Los Angeles 1 at San Jose 2 (SO)
December 26	Phoenix 3 at Los Angeles 4
December 28	Los Angeles 2 at Chicago 0
December 29	Los Angeles 0 at Winnipeg 1 (OT)
December 31	Vancouver 1 at Los Angeles 4
January 2	Colorado 2 at Los Angeles 1 (SO)
January 5	Phoenix 0 at Los Angeles 1 (OT)
January 7	Columbus 1 at Los Angeles 0
January 9	Washington 2 at Los Angeles 5
January 12	Dallas 5 at Los Angeles 4 (SO)
January 14	Los Angeles 4 at Calgary 1
January 15	Los Angeles 1 at Edmonton 2 (OT)
January 17	Los Angeles 3 at Vancouver 2 (SO)
January 19	Calgary 2 at Los Angeles 1 (SO)
January 21	Colorado 3 at Los Angeles 1
January 23	Ottawa 1 at Los Angeles 4
February 1	Columbus 2 at Los Angeles 3
February 3	Los Angeles 0 at St. Louis 1
February 4	Los Angeles 1 at Carolina 2
February 7	Los Angeles 3 at Tampa Bay 1
February 9	Los Angeles 1 at Florida 3
February 11	Los Angeles 1 at NY Islanders 2 (OT)
February 12	Los Angeles 4 at Dallas 2
February 16	Phoenix 1 at Los Angeles 0
February 18	Calgary 1 at Los Angeles 0
February 21	Los Angeles 4 at Phoenix 5 (SO)
February 22	Los Angeles 1 at Colorado 4
February 25	Chicago 0 at Los Angeles 4
February 27	Los Angeles 1 at Nashville 2
February 28	Los Angeles 4 at Minnesota 0
March 3	Anaheim 2 at Los Angeles 4
March 6	Los Angeles 5 at Nashville 4
March 8	Los Angeles 1 at Columbus 3
March 9	Los Angeles 3 at Detroit 4
March 11	Los Angeles 3 at Chicago 2 (SO)
March 13	Detroit 2 at Los Angeles 5
March 16	Los Angeles 4 at Anaheim 2
March 17	Nashville 2 at Los Angeles 4
March 20	San Jose 2 at Los Angeles 5
March 22	St. Louis 0 at Los Angeles 1 (SO)
March 24	Boston 4 at Los Angeles 2
March 26	Los Angeles 0 at Vancouver 1
March 28	Los Angeles 3 at Calgary 0
March 30	Los Angeles 4 at Edmonton 1
March 31	Los Angeles 3 at Minnesota 4 (SO)
April 2	Edmonton 0 at Los Angeles 2
April 5	San Jose 6 at Los Angeles 5 (SO)
April 7	Los Angeles 2 at San Jose 3 (OT)

Anze Kopitar led the Kings in scoring for the fourth straight season.

	GP	G	A	P	Pim
Anze Kopitar	82	25	51	76	20
Justin Williams	82	22	37	59	44
Dustin Brown	82	22	32	54	53
Mike Richards	74	18	26	44	71
Drew Doughty	77	10	26	36	69
Jeff Carter	55	21	13	34	16
Willie Mitchell	76	5	19	24	44
Jarret Stoll	78	6	15	21	60
Slava Voynov	54	8	12	20	12
Dustin Penner	65	7	10	17	43
Simon Gagne	34	7	10	17	18
Matt Greene	82	4	11	15	58
Dwight King	27	5	9	14	10
Alec Martinez	51	6	6	12	8
Kyle Clifford	81	5	7	12	123
Rob Scuderi	82	1	8	9	16
Brad Richardson	59	5	3	8	30
Colin Fraser	67	2	6	8	67
Trevor Lewis	72	3	4	7	26
Andrei Loktionov	39	3	4	7	2
Trent Hunter	38	2	5	7	8
Jordan Nolan	26	2	2	4	28
Ethan Moreau	28	1	3	4	20
Scott Parse	9	2	0	2	14
Davis Drewiske	9	2	0	2	2
Kevin Westgarth	25	1	1	2	39
Jonathan Quick	69	0	2	2	6
Jonathan Bernier	16	0	0	0	0

Goalies	GP	W–L–OT	Mins	GA	SO	GAA
Jonathan Quick	69	35–21–13	4,099:26	133	10	1.95
Jonathan Bernier	16	5–6–2	890:12	35	1	2.36

Conference Quarterfinals

Eastern Conference

(1) New York Rangers vs. (8) Ottawa

April 12	Ottawa 2 at NY Rangers 4
April 14	Ottawa 3 at NY Rangers 2 (Neil 1:17 OT)
April 16	NY Rangers 1 at Ottawa 0 [Lundqvist]
April 18	NY Rangers 2 at Ottawa 3 (Turris 2:24 OT)
April 21	Ottawa 2 at NY Rangers 0 [Anderson]
April 23	NY Rangers 3 at Ottawa 2
April 26	Ottawa 1 at NY Rangers 2

NY Rangers wins best-of-seven 4–3

(2) Boston vs. (7) Washington

April 12	Washington 0 at Boston 1 (Kelly 1:18 OT) [Thomas]
April 14	Washington 2 at Boston 1 (Backstrom 22:56 OT)
April 16	Boston 4 at Washington 3
April 19	Boston 1 at Washington 2
April 21	Washington 4 at Boston 3
April 22	Boston 4 at Washington 3 (Seguin 3:17 OT)
April 25	Washington 2 at Boston 1 (Ward 2:57 OT)

Washington wins best-of-seven 4–3

(3) Florida vs. (6) New Jersey

April 13	New Jersey 3 at Florida 2
April 15	New Jersey 2 at Florida 4
April 17	Florida 4 at New Jersey 3
April 19	Florida 0 at New Jersey 4 [Brodeur]
April 21	New Jersey 0 at Florida 3 [Theodore]
April 24	Florida 2 at New Jersey 3 (Zajac 5:39 OT)
April 26	New Jersey 3 at Florida 2 (Henrique 23:47 OT)

New Jersey wins best-of-seven 4–3

(4) Pittsburgh vs. (5) Philadelphia

April 11	Philadelphia 4 at Pittsburgh 3 (Voracek 2:23 OT)
April 13	Philadelphia 8 at Pittsburgh 5
April 15	Pittsburgh 4 at Philadelphia 8
April 18	Pittsburgh 10 at Philadelphia 3
April 20	Philadelphia 2 at Pittsburgh 3
April 22	Pittsburgh 1 at Philadelphia 5

Philadelphia wins best-of-seven 4–2

Western Conference

(1) Vancouver vs. (8) Los Angeles

April 11	Los Angeles 4 at Vancouver 2
April 13	Los Angeles 4 at Vancouver 2
April 15	Vancouver 0 at Los Angeles 1 [Quick]
April 18	Vancouver 3 at Los Angeles 1
April 22	Los Angeles 2 at Vancouver 1 (Stoll 4:27 OT)

Los Angeles wins best-of-seven 4–1

(2) St. Louis vs. (7) San Jose

April 12	San Jose 3 at St. Louis 2 (Havlat 23:34 OT)
April 14	San Jose 0 at St. Louis 3 [Halak/Elliott]
April 16	St. Louis 4 at San Jose 3
April 19	St. Louis 2 at San Jose 1
April 21	San Jose 1 at St. Louis 3

St. Louis wins best-of-seven 4–1

(3) Phoenix vs. (6) Chicago

April 12	Chicago 2 at Phoenix 3 (Hanzal 9:29 OT)
April 14	Chicago 4 at Phoenix 3 (Bickell 10:36 OT)
April 17	Phoenix 3 at Chicago 2 (Boedker 13:15 OT)
April 19	Phoenix 3 at Chicago 2 (Boedker 2:15 OT)
April 21	Chicago 2 at Phoenix 1 (Toews 2:44 OT)
April 23	Phoenix 4 at Chicago 0 [Smith]

Phoenix wins best-of-seven 4–2

(4) Nashville vs. (5) Detroit

April 11	Detroit 2 at Nashville 3
April 13	Detroit 3 at Nashville 2
April 15	Nashville 3 at Detroit 2
April 17	Nashville 3 at Detroit 1
April 20	Detroit 1 at Nashville 2

Nashville wins best-of-seven 4–1

Conference Semifinals

Eastern Conference

(1) NY Rangers vs. (7) Washington
April 28	Washington 1 at NY Rangers 3
April 30	Washington 3 at NY Rangers 2
May 2	NY Rangers 2 at Washington 1 (Gaborik 54:41 OT)
May 5	NY Rangers 2 at Washington 3
May 7	Washington 2 at NY Rangers 3 (M. Staal 1:35 OT)
May 9	NY Rangers 1 at Washington 2
May 12	Washington 1 at NY Rangers 2

NY Rangers win best-of-seven 4–3

(5) Philadelphia vs. (6) New Jersey
April 29	New Jersey 3 at Philadelphia 4 (Briere 4:36 OT)
May 1	New Jersey 4 at Philadelphia 1
May 3	Philadelphia 3 at New Jersey 4 (Ponikarovsky 17:21 OT)
May 6	Philadelphia 2 at New Jersey 4
May 8	New Jersey 3 at Philadelphia 1

New Jersey wins best-of-seven 4–1

Western Conference

(2) St. Louis vs. (8) Los Angeles
April 28	Los Angeles 3 at St. Louis 1
April 30	Los Angeles 5 at St. Louis 2
May 3	St. Louis 2 at Los Angeles 4
May 6	St. Louis 1 at Los Angeles 3

Los Angeles wins best-of-seven 4–0

(3) Phoenix vs. (4) Nashville
April 27	Nashville 3 at Phoenix 4 (Whitney 14:04 OT)
April 29	Nashville 3 at Phoenix 5
May 2	Phoenix 0 at Nashville 2 [Rinne]
May 4	Phoenix 1 at Nashville 0 [Smith]
May 7	Nashville 1 at Phoenix 2

Phoenix wins best-of-seven 4–1

Conference Finals

Eastern Conference

(1) NY Rangers vs. (6) New Jersey
May 14	New Jersey 0 at NY Rangers 3 [Lundqvist]
May 16	New Jersey 3 at NY Rangers 2
May 19	NY Rangers 3 at New Jersey 0 [Lundqvist]
May 21	NY Rangers 1 at New Jersey 4
May 23	New Jersey 5 at NY Rangers 3
May 25	NY Rangers at New Jersey
May 27	New Jersey at NY Rangers

New Jersey wins best-of-seven 4-3

Western Conference

(8) Los Angeles vs. (3) Phoenix
May 13	Los Angeles 4 at Phoenix 2
May 15	Los Angeles 4 at Phoenix 0 [Quick]
May 17	Phoenix 1 at Los Angeles 2
May 20	Phoenix 2 at Los Angeles 0 [Smith]

Los Angeles wins best-of-seven 4-0

Stanley Cup Final

(8) Los Angeles vs. (6) New Jersey
May 30	Los Angeles 2 at New Jersey 1 (OT)
June 2	Los Angeles 2 at New Jersey 1 (OT)
June 4	New Jersey 0 at Los Angeles 4
June 6	New Jersey 3 at Los Angeles 1
June 9	Los Angeles 1 at New Jersey 2
June 11	New Jersey 1 at Los Angeles 6

Los Angeles wins Stanley Cup 4–2

	GP	G	A	P	Pim
Dustin Brown	20	8	12	20	34
Anze Kopitar	20	8	12	20	9
Drew Doughty	20	4	12	16	14
Mike Richards	20	4	11	15	17
Justin Williams	20	4	11	15	12
Jeff Carter	20	8	5	13	4
Dustin Penner	20	3	8	11	32
Trevor Lewis	20	3	6	9	2
Dwight King	20	5	3	8	13
Matt Greene	20	2	4	6	12
Jarret Stoll	20	2	3	5	18
Willie Mitchell	20	1	2	3	16
Alec Martinez	20	1	2	3	8
Slava Voynov	20	1	2	3	4
Jordan Nolan	20	1	1	2	21
Colin Fraser	18	1	1	2	4
Brad Richardson	13	1	0	1	4
Rob Scuderi	20	0	1	1	4
Simon Gagne	4	0	0	0	2
Kyle Clifford	3	0	0	0	2
Jonathan Quick	20	0	0	0	0
Andrei Loktionov	2	0	0	0	0

Without sensational goaltending from Jonathan Quick, the Kings never could have made it to the Cup Final in such remarkable fashion, losing only four out of 20 postseason games.

In Goal	GP	W–L	Mins	GA	SO	GAA
Jonathan Quick	20	16–4	1,238:12	29	3	1.41

HOW THE TEAM WAS BUILT

By Draft

Jonathan Bernier
Drafted 11th overall by Los Angeles in 2006

Dustin Brown
Drafted 13th overall by Los Angeles in 2003

Kyle Clifford
Drafted 35th overall by Los Angeles in 2009

Drew Doughty
Drafted 2nd overall by Los Angeles in 2008

Dwight King
Drafted 109th overall by Los Angeles in 2007

Anze Kopitar
Drafted 11th overall by Los Angeles in 2005

Trevor Lewis
Drafted 17th overall by Los Angeles in 2006

Andrei Loktionov
Drafted 123rd overall by Los Angeles in 2008

Alec Martinez
Drafted 95th overall by Los Angeles in 2007

Jordan Nolan
Drafted 186th overall by Los Angeles in 2009

Scott Parse
Drafted 174th overall by Los Angeles in 2004

Jonathan Quick
Drafted 72nd overall by Los Angeles in 2005

Slava Voynov
Drafted 32nd overall by Los Angeles in 2008

By Free Agent Signing

Davis Drewiske
Signed as a free agent by Los Angeles on April 1, 2008

Simon Gagne
Signed as a free agent by Los Angeles on July 2, 2011

Trent Hunter
Signed as a free agent by Los Angeles on September 30, 2011

Willie Mitchell
Signed as a free agent by Los Angeles on August 25, 2010

Ethan Moreau
Signed as a free agent by Los Angeles on August 20, 2011

Rob Scuderi
Signed as a free agent by Los Angeles on July 2, 2009

Kevin Westgarth
Signed as a free agent by Los Angeles on March 16, 2007

By Trade

Jeff Carter
Acquired by Los Angeles from Columbus on February 23, 2012, for Jack Johnson and a conditional 1st-round draft choice in 2012 or 2013

Colin Fraser
Acquired by Los Angeles from Edmonton on June 26, 2011, with a 7th-round draft choice in 2012 for Ryan Smyth

Matt Greene
Acquired by Los Angeles from Edmonton on June 29, 2008, with Jarret Stoll for Lubomir Visnovsky

Dustin Penner
Acquired by Los Angeles from Edmonton on February 28, 2011, for Colton Teubert, a 1st-round draft choice in 2011, and a conditional 2nd-round draft choice in 2012

Mike Richards
Acquired by Los Angeles from Philadelphia on June 23, 2011, with Rob Bordson for Brayden Schenn, Wayne Simmonds, and a 2nd-round draft choice in 2012

Brad Richardson
Acquired by Los Angeles from Colorado on June 21, 2008, for a 2nd-round draft choice in 2008

Jarret Stoll
Acquired by Los Angeles from Edmonton on June 29, 2008, with Matt Greene for Lubomir Visnovsky

Justin Williams
Acquired by Los Angeles from Carolina on March 4, 2009, for Patrick O'Sullivan and a 2nd-round draft choice in 2009

	GP	G	A	P	Pim
Justin Azevedo	63	28	22	50	37
Brandon Kozun	74	20	26	46	58
Linden Vey	74	19	24	43	16
Marc-Andre Cliché	72	17	24	41	35
Patrick Mullen	69	13	28	41	45
Jake Muzzin	71	7	24	31	40
Dwight King	50	11	18	29	20
Thomas Hickey	76	3	23	26	36
Stefan Legein	63	14	11	25	44
David Kolomatis	58	5	20	25	12
Robert Czarnik	49	8	15	23	32
Jordan Nolan	40	9	13	22	119
Ray Kaunisto	74	7	15	22	65
Andrei Loktionov	32	5	15	20	10
Andrew Campbell	76	2	17	19	54
David Meckler	44	10	7	17	13
Richard Clune	56	6	9	15	253
Nick Deslauriers	65	1	13	14	67
Trent Hunter	20	4	6	10	8
Cam Paddock	39	2	3	5	44
Slava Voynov	15	2	2	4	4
J.D. Watt	19	2	1	3	27
Rob Mignardi	23	2	1	3	18
Justin Johnson	44	1	2	3	187
Jordan Hill	41	1	2	3	35
Brian O'Neill	12	1	1	2	4
Martin Jones	41	0	2	2	0
Andy Andreoff	5	1	0	1	4
Chris Cloud	10	0	0	0	19
Alex Hudson	15	0	0	0	9
Jeff Zatkoff	44	0	0	0	0
Joe Charlebois	11	0	0	0	0
Paul Crowder	5	0	0	0	0
Jordan Weal	2	0	0	0	0

John Zeiler of the Manchester Monarchs watches play from the bench.

Goalies	GP	W–L–OT	Mins	GA	SO	GAA
Jeff Zatkoff	44	21–17–1	2,432:26	101	3	2.49
Martin Jones	41	18–17–2	2,166:15	94	1	2.60

2012 STANLEY CUP PLAYOFFS

LA

NHL

TM

CONFERENCE QUARTERFINALS
Los Angeles Kings vs. Vancouver Canucks

GAME ONE — *APRIL 11, 2012*

Los Angeles 4 at Vancouver 2

(Los Angeles leads series 1–0)

The Kings began their 2012 playoff run in what would become trademark fashion: winning the opening game on the road to take an early series lead. The victory came as a result of their power play and a dominant third period. In the case of the former, the Kings scored two goals with the man advantage. And,

in the case of the latter, they scored the only two goals of the final period to break a 2–2 tie after 40 minutes.

The start of the game was frenetic and seemed to indicate the Canucks were ready for another march to the Stanley Cup Final. Alexandre Burrows opened the scoring when he got a second chance in the slot, burying a shot past a screened Jonathan Quick to send the hometown crowd into a frenzy.

The Kings recovered, first by killing off a penalty and then by tying the game on a power play of their

Vancouver goalie Roberto Luongo smothers the puck while the Kings look for a rebound.

Jeff Carter celebrates Mike Richards' tying goal in the first period of Game 1.

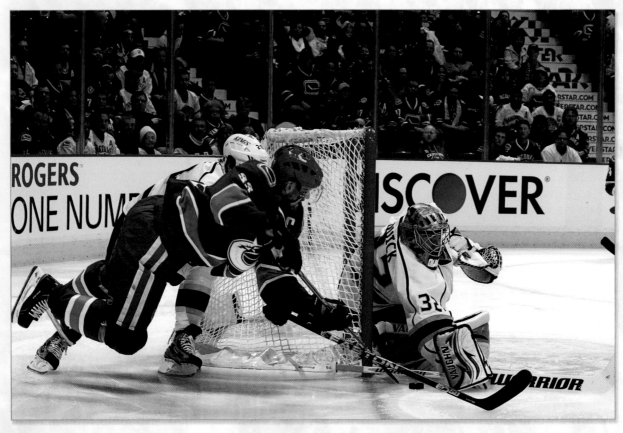

Vancouver captain Henrik Sedin tries a wraparound, but goalie Jonathan Quick is there to prevent the goal.

own. The goal proved to be a huge turning point in the series. Goalie Roberto Luongo looked awkward, allowing Mike Richards' shot to squeeze through him from a bad angle. Luongo, the fans, and the Kings immediately sensed the Canucks' netminder was not on his game.

The contest went more than 23 minutes without another goal. Quick held the visitors in the game during this stretch as the Canucks threw all their offensive power at the Kings. Late in the second period, Los Angeles took a 2–1 lead on another power play. During a Canucks' five-minute major, the result of a Byron Bitz boarding call, Willie Mitchell hammered a point shot through traffic that found the back of the net.

Not to be outdone, the Canucks tied the game with 7.3 seconds left in the middle frame. The Kings were called for icing late in a shift and couldn't change lines. After the ensuing faceoff, Alexander Edler's point shot found its way through a maze of players and past the goaltender.

Undaunted by the often debilitating effects of a late goal, the Kings came out and took control of the game in the third period. They didn't allow the Canucks much of a chance to get the crowd back into the game, even though Vancouver had the only two power plays of the final frame. Los Angeles killed those off in fine fashion and then scored the go-ahead goal with just 3:14 left in regulation. Jeff Carter made a sensational play as he had a pass come behind him while he headed to the net. He managed to redirect the puck off his back skate, past Edler and onto the stick of Dustin Penner, who had an open side and didn't miss. The goal silenced the once-raucous crowd.

Dustin Brown added an empty-net goal to seal the victory with 17.9 seconds remaining, and the Kings claimed home-ice advantage with the road win.

"I wasn't so much worried about us getting frustrated so much as letting one slip away," Penner said. "We got a fortunate bounce on my goal, but we worked hard for 60 minutes tonight and it worked out for us."

GAME TWO — *APRIL 13, 2012*

Los Angeles 4 at Vancouver 2
(Los Angeles leads series 2–0)

Friday the 13th was a nightmare for the Vancouver Canucks. Game 1 of the series had been close for the first 55 minutes, but this game was well under the Kings' control by early in the second period. The Canucks were unable to use their fan support or superior regular-season record to ignite a comeback. They lost their second straight game at Rogers Arena, giving the Kings a comfortable lead heading to California for Game 3.

In Game 1, the Kings power play was the difference. In Game 2 it was their penalty killing which played a pivotal role in the outcome, as captain Dustin Brown scored two short-handed goals. The first came at 19:51 of the first period and would prove to be a psychological back-breaker for the Canucks.

On a Vancouver power play with time running out in the period, Anze Kopitar made a sensational poke check off Alexander Edler at the blue line. Kopitar rushed to the net and tried a great move in close, but Roberto Luongo managed to make the stop. However, the rebound came to Brown in the slot and, with bodies crowding the net, he managed to wrist a shot through everyone and into the goal with just 8.6 seconds left in the period.

Vancouver recovered after the intermission, tying the score on the opening shift when a Henrik Sedin point shot was tipped in front by Jannik Hansen just 17 seconds into the period. That great start was undone just five minutes later on another

Trevor Lewis of Los Angeles prepares for a faceoff against Manny Malhotra.

Conference Quarterfinals – Los Angeles Kings vs. Vancouver Canucks

25

Manny Malhotra (left) and Matt Greene collide along the boards during Game 2.

Conference Quarterfinals – Los Angeles Kings vs. Vancouver Canucks

home-team power play. Ryan Kesler's pass back to the point went by defenceman Dan Hamhuis and Brown claimed the loose puck at the blue line. He went in alone on Luongo, made a nice deke, and a great opportunity for Vancouver to take the lead now saw the Kings go up 2–1. It was a lead they never relinquished.

Brown's second shorty tied an NHL record (set 12 previous times) for most shorthanded goals in a playoff game.

"It was important for our top guys to lead by example," Brown said. "You need big performances at this time of year."

Vancouver's problems were exacerbated by the play of Jonathan Quick in the Los Angeles goal. It was tough enough to penetrate the Kings' defence, but when they did manage to get established in the offensive zone, the Canucks simply couldn't beat the reliable Quick.

Midway through the final period, on a Kings power play, Jarret Stoll banged in a loose puck past a seated Luongo to extend the lead and give Brown another point on the night. A few minutes later, Trevor Lewis intercepted a weak pass from Alexandre Burrows behind the Canucks' goal and wrapped the puck in to seal the victory and silence the home crowd once and for all. A late goal from Samuel Pahlsson only made the score a bit closer.

"Five-on-five we played well," suggested Vancouver captain Henrik Sedin. "The power play is not good enough right now. Not only are we not scoring, but we're giving up goals. That can't happen. That's why we lost the game."

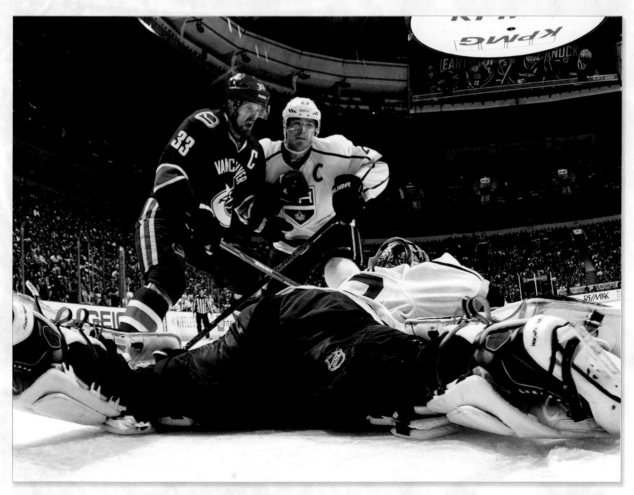

Jonathan Quick makes a save while captains Henrik Sedin (left) and Dustin Brown fight for space.

GAME THREE — APRIL 15, 2012

Vancouver 0 at **Los Angeles 1**
(Los Angeles leads series 3–0)

Los Angeles captain Dustin Brown continued to lead by example and goalie Jonathan Quick continued to block everything in sight. These two elements combined to allow Los Angeles a 1–0 victory in Game 3, putting Vancouver's postseason on the ropes. It was an unexpected start to the playoffs given that the Canucks had more points, more wins, and more goals than the Kings over the 82-game regular season.

Brown scored his fourth goal of the series at 6:30 of the third period and Quick stopped all 41 shots in the victory. Los Angeles generated only 20 shots of their own against Vancouver's Cory Schneider.

"This team's been trying to put pieces together for the past five or six years," Brown said. "It's been a long road, and I think it's really just starting for this team. Going into the series, does this group believe we could have beat them? Definitely. We never thought we were going be up 3–0 in this series against a team that's pretty well dominated this League for the last two years. In saying that, it's three games. It takes four to win."

Vancouver coach Alain Vigneault was so desperate to get something going for his team – and so disappointed in the performance of No. 1 goalie Roberto Luongo – that he started Schneider for the crucial third game. And while the Canucks still lost, it certainly wasn't because of suspect goaltending.

"We had many opportunities. We didn't get it done," Vigneault said succinctly afterward.

Dustin Brown scores the winning goal in Game 3 after being left alone at the back side of the play.

Zack Kassian brings the puck out front, but goalie Jonathan Quick covers the short side and keeps it out.

"Getting it done" referred, in large measure, to the team's power play. It went 0-for-4 in Game 3, making it 0-for-14 in the series, a number not nearly good enough for a team that had Stanley Cup ambitions.

"They've been hard-fought games that could have gone either way [and] haven't gone either way," said Vigneault. "Give them credit. They're up and we're in that tough position right now."

But for a bounce here or there, the game might have been different. Jannik Hansen beat Quick with a shot midway through the first period, but it rang hard off the post and stayed out. Then, with one second left in the period, Quick stopped a back-door shot from Alexandre Burrows.

In the second period, the Canucks dominated but went to the dressing room after 40 minutes still in a 0–0 game. Then, as overtime seemed a distinct possibility, Justin Williams took a shot from the faceoff circle that Schneider kicked out. The puck went right to Brown, who drilled it high into the open side of the net for the game's first – and only – goal.

Conference Quarterfinals – Los Angeles Kings vs. Vancouver Canucks

29

Captain Dustin Brown celebrates his crucial goal in Game 3, which gave the Kings a commanding 3–0 lead in the series.

GAME FOUR — APRIL 18, 2012

Vancouver 3 at Los Angeles 1

(Los Angeles leads series 3–1)

Everything that was supposed to go right for Vancouver did, and the Canucks avoided the ignominy of a first-round sweep by coming up with an impressive 3–1 road win to send the series back to Rogers Arena for Game 5. Daniel Sedin was back in the lineup after a nearly month-long absence due to a concussion; goalie Cory Schneider was excellent, stopping 43 of 44 shots, including a penalty shot with the game's outcome still very much in the balance; and the Canucks finally got a power-play goal.

"They've got a lot of pressure on them," said Daniel's twin brother, Henrik. "Being up, 3–0, they wanted to finish it off here. Now we'll bring it back to Vancouver, and we'll focus on one game. If we can take that, it's a new series."

The first period did not start well for the visitors, however, as Los Angeles had the only goal of the opening 20 minutes. Anze Kopitar easily got around a defending Mason Raymond and beat Schneider with a great shot to make it a 1–0 game. A series sweep seemed like a distinct possibility.

But Alexander Edler responded with Vancouver's first power-play goal of the series at 4:07 of the second period when his seemingly harmless point shot found its way past a scrum of bodies and in. It was a fortunate goal, the kind the Canucks hadn't managed to get in the first three games of the series. Less than five minutes later, Kevin Bieksa gave the

Willie Mitchell of the Kings demonstrates what playoff hockey is all about, lunging for a puck to prevent it from coming to Ryan Kesler.

Conference Quarterfinals – Los Angeles Kings vs. Vancouver Canucks

31

Kings and Canucks players battle tenaciously in front of Vancouver goalie Cory Schneider, but the puck stays out.

Canucks a 2–1 lead after the team capitalized on a turnover by Mike Richards outside the blue line. Bieksa's shot tipped off Richards' stick in front of the net and past a helpless Jonathan Quick.

Vancouver had an early power play in the third period, but Dustin Brown stole the puck from Bieksa at the Kings' blue line and went in alone on Schneider. Bieksa tripped up Brown, resulting in a penalty shot. The Canucks' goaltender wasn't fooled by Brown's deke and made the save as the shot came off the captain's forehand. The stop put the game firmly in the Canucks' hands.

"He came out really far, so I didn't really see much to shoot at," Brown said. "He bit on the first fake, but he had a good push off . . . I tried to slide it by. It wasn't there."

Seconds later, the Canucks continued their power play – and capitalized. Henrik Sedin made it 3–1 after he dazzled in the corner, got the puck to the point, and batted a rebound out of the air to earn a two-goal lead. The Canucks went on to win, but there was still plenty of work to be done before they could celebrate.

And the Kings? They had to regroup and realize a 3–1 series lead was still a good position to be in.

The atmosphere was electric at the STAPLES Center prior to Game 4 in Los Angeles.

Conference Quarterfinals – Los Angeles Kings vs. Vancouver Canucks

33

GAME FIVE — *APRIL 13, 2012*

Los Angeles 2 at Vancouver 1 (OT)

(Los Angeles wins series 4–1)

In 2011, Vancouver went to Game 7 of the Stanley Cup Final before succumbing to the Boston Bruins. In 2012, the team went home after only five playoff games. The Presidents' Trophy winners and defending Western Conference champion Canucks were eliminated by a Jarret Stoll overtime goal. It was the first playoff series win for the Kings in 11 years.

"To be honest, it doesn't matter if you lose the seventh game of the Final or you lose in five in the first round – it's devastating," Vancouver's Daniel Sedin admitted. "We have the mindset to win every year. When you end up on the losing side, it's tough. We've got to come back and be stronger."

In the other dressing room, the mood wasn't euphoric so much as satisfied. "It's been a long road for a lot of guys in here that have been in this organization and put in a lot of time and just coming together as a group and to finally take a – this is just one step – but to take a step in this playoff atmosphere is huge for this team," said Los Angeles captain Dustin Brown. "I'm just proud of this group."

Playing at home, the Canucks seemed to be getting on track, using the momentum from their Game 4 win to get off to a great start in Game 5. The Kings failed to score on two early power plays, and then Henrik Sedin got to a rebound in close on a Vancouver power play.

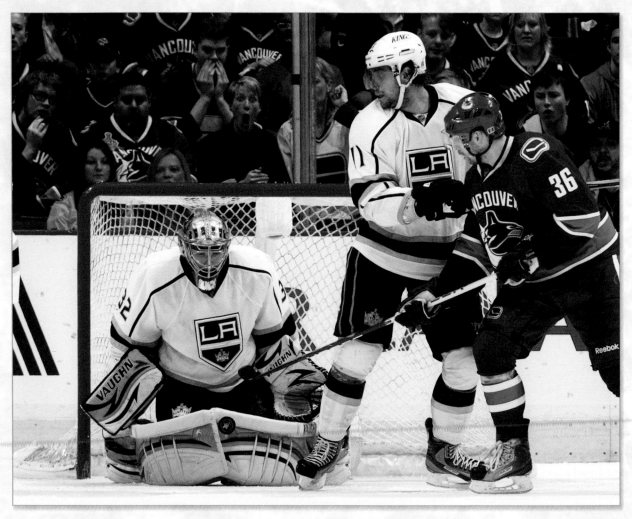

Goalie Jonathan Quick makes the save while teammate Anze Kopitar prevents Vancouver forward Jannik Hansen from getting a rebound.

Brad Richardson scores a goal to even the score as Henrik Sedin unsuccessfully tries to tie him up and Alexander Edler can't stop the puck from entering the net.

Conference Quarterfinals – Los Angeles Kings vs. Vancouver Canucks

35

The Kings celebrate their Game 5 win, which eliminated the Canucks from Vancouver from the playoffs and took Los Angeles to the Western Conference Semifinals.

That 1–0 goal midway through the first would stand for nearly 30 minutes.

The opening frame ended dramatically, as Anze Kopitar had a breakaway with the clock winding down. His shot was stopped by Cory Schneider right at the buzzer, but it was clear Kopitar would have skated in closer had he had a few more seconds to work with.

Both teams had plenty of great chances in the second period. Daniel Sedin had a clear breakaway but was stopped by Jonathan Quick, while Schneider was a wall at the other end, working as the No. 1 penalty killer against the Kings' two power plays.

Early in the third, things turned better for Los Angeles. Defenceman Drew Doughty rushed the puck down the right wing after picking up an errant pass at centre ice. As the Canucks waited for him to pass, he kept gliding toward the corner. Just as it looked like

he would curl behind the net, Doughty snuck the puck into the crease, where Brad Richardson lifted a quick shot over Schneider for the tying score.

Early in overtime, Vancouver's Dan Hamhuis was hounded mercilessly by Trevor Lewis as he tried to carry the puck out of his own end. He gave it up at his blue line, and Stoll took it down the left wing. The right-handed centre had a great angle and beat Schneider with a quick shot to the short side, sending the Kings into the next round and the 2011 Stanley Cup finalists home.

"[Lewis] made a great play to force the turnover and it was a quick 2-on-1 with [rookie Dwight] King, and I was shooting all the way," Stoll said. "I saw a little room up top and put it where I wanted to. I just got lucky, I guess."

36

Conference Quarterfinals – Los Angeles Kings vs. Vancouver Canucks

GAME ONE — APRIL 28, 2012

Los Angeles 3 at St. Louis 1

(Los Angeles leads series 1–0)

Goalie Jonathan Quick had climbed near the top of the list of early Conn Smythe Trophy candidates with his play through the Kings' first-round victory, and he continued his dominant play in the second-round opener against the Blues. The young netminder was clearly the difference as Los Angeles took another 1–0 series lead on the road.

"That's the advantage of having a guy like that in the net," said captain Dustin Brown of his goalie. "Early in the game, we needed him to make some big saves, and he did. We grinded the rest of the game out and got a 'W.'"

Indeed, although the Blues led 1–0 midway through the opening period, it could have been a much larger lead if not for Quick's play. He robbed Andy McDonald from in close during the first minute and continued to be rock solid until a deflected David Backes point shot made its way through several players to give St. Louis the opening goal at 9:16.

The Blues continued to press, but couldn't get a second puck past Quick. The Kings slowly gained their footing, buoyed by their goalie's strength of will. With just 3:02 left in the period, they tied the game. Dustin Penner made a sensational pass from the corner of the Blues' end through traffic in front of the net. Slava Voynov, sneaking in from the far side, took the pass, and snapped home a one-timer before the Blues knew what had happened. Now, despite the lopsided edge in play, St. Louis was going to the dressing room tied, 1–1.

"We were able to kind of weather the storm a little bit," Quick said, downplaying his role. "They got one early, but we were able to get one back at the end

Goalie Jonathan Quick stares down St. Louis forward Alexander Steen from point-blank range.

Western Conference Semifinals – Los Angeles Kings vs. St. Louis Blues

37

of the first and we continued strong play through the last two periods. Whenever you're on the road, no matter what time of the year it is, you expect the other team to come out flying in the first 10 minutes on home ice like that. This team is no different, obviously. They're one of the best teams on home ice for a reason, and that first 10 minutes really put us on our heels for a little bit. But, we weathered the storm and were able to tie it up at the end of the first."

The Kings took the lead late in the second in what was becoming trademark fashion. Playing short-handed with a faceoff deep in the Kings' own end, Brown got to a loose puck in the circle and headed up ice on a two-on-two. He barrelled in on goalie Brian Elliott, who made a pad save. But no one had taken the trailer Greene who lifted the rebound in at 18:57 to make it 2–1 for the visitors.

The Blues threw everything they had at the Kings in the final period, but the only other goal came from Penner, who put one into an open net with 15 seconds left in the game. St. Louis, like Vancouver, had squandered home-ice advantage and now faced a must-win situation in Game 2.

"When you play Los Angeles, there's a price to pay to win," St. Louis coach Ken Hitchcock said. "There's a high price to pay. If we expect to win the next game, we're going to have to pay a bigger price than the one we paid. I don't just mean physical play. I mean, they defend well, they keep you to the outside, they've got big defencemen and what happened in the first period was we got to the inside, we worked hard to get there and then we allowed ourselves to stay to the outside. Once they got the 2–1 lead, they kept everything to the outside, and we shot ourselves in the foot in the third period with penalties."

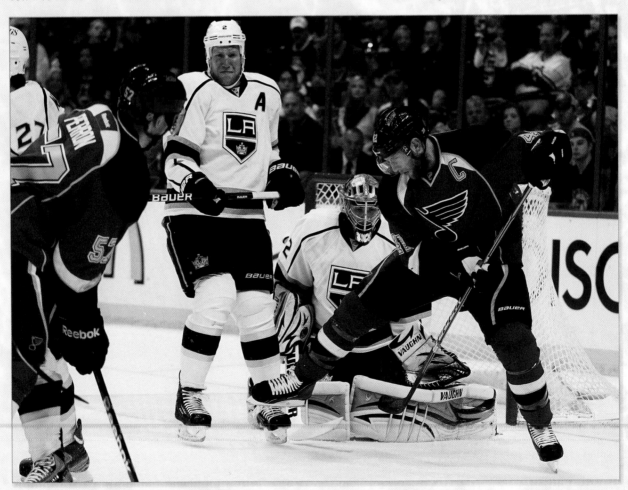

Los Angeles defenceman Matt Greene grimaces as a shot on goal passes St. Louis forward David Backes, who nimbly gets out of the way.

Taking it all in stride, the Kings celebrate their road win in Game 1 against the Blues.

Western Conference Semifinals – Los Angeles Kings vs. St. Louis Blues

39

GAME TWO — *APRIL 30, 2012*

Los Angeles 5 at St. Louis 2

(Los Angeles leads series 2–0)

The Kings launched an all-out attack in the first period, scoring four unanswered goals to gain control of the game and the series. The Kings' success was as shocking to the second-seeded Blues as it had been for the first-place Canucks in the previous round.

The onslaught began just 31 seconds after the opening faceoff. Dustin Penner came out of the corner deep in the St. Louis end and went hard to the net. Brian Elliott made the save on the attempted stuff-in, but Mike Richards was right there to lift the rebound in.

The score stayed at 1–0 for the better part of 14 minutes, but then Dustin Brown did what he does best – set up goals with his team shorthanded. Brown intercepted a pass mid-air inside the St. Louis end, controlled the puck and fired across ice to a streaking Anze Kopitar, who moved in on Elliott. Kopitar made a sensational deke and jammed the puck in for a 2–0 lead.

"We were putting some pretty good pressure on their defence," Kopitar said. "I was kind of reading the play and ready to jump in. The instincts kicked in. The way it went in, I was pretty happy with it. A pretty big goal, I guess."

The floodgates opened in the final 90 seconds of the period. Jeff Carter came down the right wing on a chance that was anything but dangerous. His shot was blocked in front, but the puck came right back to him and he fired again. The second attempt went through the bodies in front and found its way into the back of the net at 18:37.

Dustin Brown tries to create some room in front of St. Louis goalie Brian Elliott as defenceman Roman Polak looks on.

40

Western Conference Semifinals – Los Angeles Kings vs. St. Louis Blues

Just over a minute later, the Kings made it 4–0 when Kopitar went to the net unchecked and got his stick on a great pass from Justin Williams. That brought out the boo-birds in St. Louis and pretty much wrapped up the game. Shots had favoured Los Angeles 16–5 in the first, a stat that was indicative of the dominance the visitors enjoyed in the opening period.

"We got off to a good start," Brown acknowledged. "Scoring 30 seconds into the game helps. We didn't let off the gas at all."

Andy McDonald made it a 4–1 game just 18 seconds into the second, but rather than start a comeback, the goal merely reminded the Kings of the task at hand. A minute later, Williams made it 5–1 when he lifted a loose puck past Elliott.

Matt D'Agostini got the only goal of the third to make it 5–2, but it was too little, too late. The Kings had won this game in the opening period, and there was no way they were going to lose a big lead in the final 20 minutes.

The victory gave the Kings a chance to close out the series with two wins on home ice. They were now 5–0 on the road in the playoffs and, after going without a goal in nine scoring chances, the Blues were 0-for-12 in the series with a man advantage.

"We have a big challenge ahead of us," said Quick. "We know they are going to come out hard in Game 3 and we've got to be ready."

"They scored four goals. It was pretty easy," St. Louis coach Ken Hitchcock observed. "They were full marks. They checked us hard. They checked us hard and we coughed up the puck. We made mistakes. The playoffs is one loss, so you move on. I think there are some obvious things we have to address."

Goalie Jonathan Quick loses sight of the puck, but teammates Matt Greene and Mike Richards come to his aid and prevent a goal.

Western Conference Semifinals – Los Angeles Kings vs. St. Louis Blues

41

Kings forward Jeff Carter is crunched along the boards by Alexander Steen and Barret Jackman.

GAME THREE — MAY 3, 2012

St. Louis 2 at Los Angeles 4

(Los Angeles leads series 3–0)

Once again the Kings rose to the occasion. For every challenge they faced, they came up with an answer. For every great play by their opponents, they had two great plays. They created a formula that worked and they executed their game plan to perfection. Jonathan Quick was great in goal again. The Kings scored first again. They responded to a St. Louis threat again. And as a result, they skated off the ice with a solid 4–2 win to create a virtually insurmountable 3–0 series lead.

"Winning obviously does that for you, especially in the playoffs, and the way we've done it – we've kept with our system, we've played well in a lot of situations that we've been put in," Mike Richards said. "It's enabled us to go out there and play the same system, the same game we've played all year. It gives us confidence and helps us have success, too."

As their game-opening goal showed yet again, the Kings did things with remarkable simplicity. They had possession in the St. Louis end without looking particularly dangerous. But defenceman Drew Doughty then moved in and made an aggressive and confident pass to Justin Williams, who was in the slot but surrounded by Blues. Williams wasted no time in getting his shot off, and goalie Brian Elliott wasn't prepared for what looked like a pass. The puck squirted over the goal line, and Los Angeles had another first-period lead.

The Blues tied the game early in the second. Kris Russell came over the Los Angeles blue line and dished the puck off to a charging Chris Stewart. Quick

Vladimir Sobotka of the Blues comes out front with the puck while being watched by goalie Jonathan Quick and hounded by defenceman Matt Greene.

Western Conference Semifinals – Los Angeles Kings vs. St. Louis Blues

43

Justin Williams celebrates a goal from teammate Dwight King as the puck gets by Brian Elliott.

couldn't close his pads quick enough and Stewart's backhander snuck through to make it a 1–1 game at 1:13 of the middle period.

But as the Kings had proved before, such a goal was not a setback, merely a small event in the bigger picture. On the very next play, the Kings' Matt Greene just barely got the puck out of his own end, but it ended up passing three Blues players. A speedy Dwight King got to it first along the right-wing boards. He fired a quick shot that caught Elliott off guard, and the Blues again lost momentum.

The Kings increased the lead to 3–1 on a goal Elliott would have liked to have back. On the power play, Drew Doughty got the puck down low to Richards and, from a bad angle, he fired a shot on goal that snuck between the pads of the goalie as he hugged the post. It was the kind of goal the Blues simply couldn't afford to give a Kings team that had proved so resilient and so effective playing with the

lead. It was the team's first power-play goal in 31 chances.

"I got a little lucky there," Richards admitted. "It squeaked through, and I don't even think it hit the back of the net, but it's something that feels great right now."

The last hope for the Blues came early in the third when Stewart got his second of the game on a fine effort. Quick made a lunging pad save from a left-wing shot, but the puck came free and Stewart dove to get his stick on the puck while being checked in front. That made it 3–2, but the confident Kings neither panicked nor collapsed.

Instead, less than four minutes later they doubled their lead once more. On a play that looked like a 1980s Oilers' Gretzky-to-Coffey goal, Richards came down the right side, stopped, and waited for the trailer on the play, Doughty. Richards made a perfect pass, and Doughty ripped a hard shot in to seal the win and put a stranglehold on the series.

The Kings celebrate another win in Game 3 to give them a 3–0 series lead against St. Louis.

GAME FOUR — MAY 6, 2012

St. Louis 1 at **Los Angeles 3**
(Los Angeles wins series 4–0)

Another early goal, another comeback squashed before it could become dangerous, another win, and another series out of the way. The Los Angeles Kings may have been a middling eighth in the Western Conference during the regular season, but they were playing like champions in the postseason.

"It's the time of the year when you have to enjoy hockey," goalie Jonathan Quick said. "It's the time of the year when you don't know if you are going to have another game, so you just try to enjoy every day and try to enjoy the game as much as you can."

The Kings opened the scoring again with another harmless play that they converted into a scoring chance. Roman Polak of St. Louis lost the puck in the corner and it skittered into the slot where Jordan Nolan ripped a shot past Brian Elliott before the goalie knew what was happening. The tally sent the hometown crowd into a frenzy as a sweep was now closer to reality.

The one moment of hope for the Blues came at 11:34 of the first. Barret Jackman caught the Kings on a dreadful line change and moved the puck quickly up the boards to Kevin Shattenkirk, who was in all alone. His long shot rattled off the far post and past Quick to tie the game. But for the Kings, poise was their middle name. The goal had no impact on their game and they stuck to their system as they had since entering the postseason.

Later in the first, yet another rush of seemingly little consequence turned into a pivotal moment. Anze Kopitar hit linemate Dustin Brown with a pass in the centre-ice area, and Brown skated down the left wing.

Goalie Jonathan Quick can't get to the puck, but it trickles just wide of the goal.

Los Angeles defenceman Drew Doughty collides with Andy McDonald along the boards.

He was checked by Alex Pietrangelo, but still managed to get a shot off. The defenceman worked as a screen and the puck went top corner over Elliott's glove. It wasn't the hardest shot, but it was perfectly accurate.

The game was tense the rest of the way, as the Kings played with a determination that is the very embodiment of playoff hockey. Brown added his second goal into an empty net to seal the win, give the Kings a four-game sweep, and advance the team to the Western Conference Final for the first time since 1993, when they were captained by Wayne Gretzky.

"We knew we had all the ingredients in here to make something special happen, and it's coming together," Jarrett Stoll said. "But we're only halfway there. We got a long ways to go yet. But we're getting closer. Any time you knock off a team the calibre of the St. Louis Blues, you're doing something right."

Brown shared those sentiments: "I've been here a long time, and it's one of those I've been waiting to be in this situation, continue on. I'm pretty excited right now, but you wake up tomorrow and you realize you're just halfway done."

It was the first time in Kings history that they had swept a seven-game series.

It's all over. The Kings sweep the Blues to advance to the Western Conference Final after playing only nine games in the first two rounds of the playoffs.

GAME ONE — *MAY 13, 2012*
Los Angeles 4 at Phoenix 2
(Los Angeles leads series 1–0)

Another road game and another win for the Kings, who were starting their third playoff series as the visitors but who now had a record of 6–0 away from home in the 2012 playoffs.

In the Western Conference Final, the Kings faced a resilient team that had a feel-good story to challenge their own. The Phoenix Coyotes had been playing well for the last few seasons, but had never been considered favourites to advance far into the playoffs. Yet here they were, ready to challenge the Kings for a spot in the Final.

The first two periods saw teams exchange goals, but just as with the postseason opener against the Canucks, the Kings took a 2–2 tie after 40 minutes and turned it into a 4–2 road win after 60. And as had so often been the case this year, Dustin Brown was the hero at one end and Jonathan Quick at the other.

Anze Kopitar opened the scoring for the Kings less than four minutes into the game when he picked up a loose puck in the slot and beat goalie Mike Smith with a high backhand. Smith had been the same rock in net for the Coyotes that Quick was for L.A., but on the Kopitar shot, he was screened and had little chance.

"Right before the game [head coach] Darryl made sure to tell us the first five minutes are so important, we need to be the fastest team, the hardest-working team, we want them not to want to play us," Drew Doughty said. "I thought we did a good job of that."

The Kings dominated the period, but were unable to beat Smith and increase their lead. And then, with

Coyotes forward Mikkel Boedker prepares to take a bad-angle shot while goalie Jonathan Quick is in position.

Western Conference Final – Los Angeles Kings vs. Phoenix Coyotes

49

6:34 left in the period, Phoenix defenceman Derek Morris fired a shot on goal from exactly centre ice. Quick was slightly out of position and clearly not ready for the 100-foot shot, which beat him cleanly to the far side.

"It skipped off the ice, took a weird hop, and nothing you can do about it," Quick said. "You just reset and get ready for the next shot, that's all it is." The Kings knew they wouldn't be playing in the Conference Final without Quick and were able to support him, through words of encouragement and their own play. "I think we just felt we have to get a couple for Quickie," Kopitar said. "He was bailing us out all season and a few times in the playoffs, too. I don't think anybody was concerned or worried about it. We just kind of looked at each other and said maybe we should win this one for him."

The Kings took another lead eight minutes into the second as they took advantage of a turnover at centre ice. Mike Richards and Dwight King went in on a two-on-one, and while Richards' shot was stopped by Smith, King poked in the rebound to make it 2–1 for the visitors.

Late in the period, the Coyotes again tied the score by creating something out of nothing. Quick played the puck behind his goal to defenceman Drew Doughty, who was immediately checked. Shane Doan came in and got it, whipped a pass out front to Mikkel Boedker, who fired it in to make it 2–2 at 18:05.

But the ever-resilient Kings came out all business to start the final period and Brown put the Kings up by a goal for the third time in the game just 2:11 in. Slava Voynov hit Brown with a perfect pass as he was breaking up the middle. The captain let go a terrific shot that Smith couldn't block.

"That was a great pass by Slava," Doughty offered. "I think everyone knows he has that vision offensively to do those kinds of things. Right away he saw Brownie before he even got the puck, and from there he made a great pass and Brownie finished it off from there."

King added his second of the night into the empty net for the game's final goal.

Jarret Stoll makes an extra effort to get a shot away, but Mike Smith is there to make the save.

A close call for Jonathan Quick sees the puck fly out of his reach but, luckily, off the crossbar.

Western Conference Final – Los Angeles Kings vs. Phoenix Coyotes

51

GAME TWO — MAY 15, 2012

Los Angeles 4 at Phoenix 0
(Los Angeles leads series 2–0)

The Kings' brilliance away from the STAPLES Center continued as Los Angeles ran its record to 7–0 on the road in the 2012 playoffs. The hero was, as usual, goalie Jonathan Quick, who made 24 saves and posted a shutout. Forward Jeff Carter, a mid-season acquisition from Columbus, had a standout performance as well, recording a hat trick.

"It's a mind-set; we get away, there are no distractions," Carter said. "For some reason, this team likes to play on the road."

The only goal Carter didn't score during Game 2 was the first one. Like so many of the Kings' goals in the playoffs, it came from a play that looked harmless.

Los Angeles got the puck into the Phoenix end and the puck came around the boards to Drew Doughty at the point. His quick shot was on net, but a group of bodies plugged the crease effectively. Dwight King managed to redirect the puck off the post and in. Phoenix goalie Mike Smith had absolutely no chance on the play.

Carter's first of the game came early in the second period. Mike Richards was checked in the corner, but the puck came to the side of the Coyotes goal and bounced in front. Carter was being checked but got his stick on the puck and knocked it in. Another seemingly innocent play ended up with the puck in the back of the net.

"It was huge, especially because we didn't have the best start," Kopitar said of the 2–0 goal. "We were up in shots, but we were in and out of their zone the

Los Angeles captain Dustin Brown gets out of the way of a check from the Coyotes' Rostislav Klesla.

52

Western Conference Final – Los Angeles Kings vs. Phoenix Coyotes

Mike Richards and Antoine Vermette prepare for a faceoff.

Although he is closely checked, Kings forward Jeff Carter manages to score to make it 2–0 for Los Angeles.

whole time. Quickie held us in it again and we were able to get our legs underneath us and push through. Getting the second goal and obviously getting the PP goal was huge for us to get more insurance. After that we brought it home safe."

Be that as it may, the Coyotes were down 2–0 and couldn't afford to lose their second home game in a row. Yet for all the desperation Phoenix brought to the rest of the game, the Kings were that much better. The Coyotes came apart at the seams, spending much of the rest of the game in the penalty box.

Phoenix captain Shane Doan was given a major penalty, a 10-minute misconduct, and a game misconduct at the same time Daymond Langkow was given a minor for slashing. Carter made it 3–0 on the ensuing five-on-three power play when he redirected an Anze Kopitar shot from the high slot. The goal ended the comeback hopes of the Coyotes.

Carter got another five-on-three goal midway through the final period when he smacked home a

loose puck to the side of the goal. Martin Hanzal had been given a five-minute major and game misconduct to help tee up the advantage for the Kings.

"We really want it right now," admitted Dustin Penner. "We want the first goal. We want the next goal. It's that intensity and that passion that drives us. It's that good type of fear that stops you from letting games get away from you and continues to push you forward. We use that fear of losing to motivate us as opposed to shrinking to it."

"We have to keep going. We have to keep finishing our checks," Los Angeles captain Dustin Brown said. "When you have everyone, whether it's your best players or your role players, finishing checks, doing everything they can to get in the way, it can get frustrating (for the other team). The intensity is high, and at this stage of the playoffs it's important to understand that if they are frustrated we have to keep doing what we're doing."

GAME THREE — MAY 17, 2012

Phoenix 1 at **Los Angeles 2**
(Los Angeles leads series 3–0)

For the third time in as many series, the Kings took an overwhelming 3–0 lead in the best-of-seven, virtually assuring victory. In Game 3, they played with the poise they had maintained throughout the postseason as they had to come from behind for the win.

"There's a lot of guys that haven't experienced this and a lot of guys that have," said Kings captain Dustin Brown. "The thing that's made us successful as a team is handling that success. We've put ourselves up 3–0 again. It's not only an opportunity but now a responsibility to prepare ourselves to have a good game."

The opening period was scoreless, but not without some tense moments at both ends of the ice. Both teams knew what was at stake: a Coyotes win would put them right back in the series; a loss would be devastating.

Phoenix opened the scoring just 1:03 into the second period when Daymond Langkow received a great pass from Keith Yandle. Langkow burst in on goal and beat Jonathan Quick with a shot that skittered between his pads and over the goal line. It was the first time all series that Phoenix had a lead.

But the Kings never allowed a goal to upset them and they always had the knack of coming back quickly. Just two minutes later, the Kings tied the game on a similar play. This time it was Brown who fired a great pass up the middle to a streaking Anze Kopitar, who

Dwight King loses his balance to the side of the Phoenix net as Coyotes players protect their goalie, Mike Smith.

Western Conference Final – Los Angeles Kings vs. Phoenix Coyotes

55

skated in alone and calmly made a deke on Mike Smith before tucking the puck between the goalie's pads as he slid back into the net.

"It's obviously great to limit their momentum," Dwight King noted. "It's great to see the guys capitalize when the opportunities come. We didn't have a great start and for [Kopitar] to get that goal and tie it up, that was great for our team."

The Kings took the lead early in the third after a Phoenix turnover at centre ice led to Los Angeles applying great pressure in the Coyotes' end. Los Angeles cycled and controlled the puck, banged bodies and made life difficult for the Coyotes, eventually drawing a penalty. As Quick skated to the bench for the extra attacker, King skated out of the

corner unmolested and roofed a hard shot over the glove of Smith to make it 2–1.

Given the composure needed at this time, the Coyotes displayed a lack of discipline, incurring the only three penalties in the final period. Los Angeles couldn't increase its lead, but Phoenix also couldn't gain the needed momentum or keep up a sustained attack. The result was a commanding series lead for the Kings.

"We know what we have to do. We have to win the next game," offered Coyotes captain Shane Doan. "I mean, that's all. We have to play better and find a way to win the next one. . . . We're disappointed we're down 3–0, but this is a pretty resilient group – got to find a way to win the next game."

Dwight King celebrates his third-period goal, which turned out to be the game-winner, giving the Kings their third 3–0 lead in games in as many series.

Willie Mitchell (black) and Antoine Vermette battle for precious space on ice.

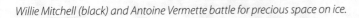

Western Conference Final – Los Angeles Kings vs. Phoenix Coyotes

57

GAME FOUR — MAY 20, 2012

Phoenix 2 at Los Angeles 0

(Los Angeles leads series 3–1)

In Game 4, things finally went the Coyotes' way and the Kings proved mere mortals capable of the odd slip. Phoenix won the game doing exactly what they had to do. They got the better goaltending. They got timely goals. And, they prevented the Kings from getting back into the game.

"I think tonight was more about the Phoenix Coyotes playing a good game," said Los Angeles captain Dustin Brown. "They sat back and they are opportunistic and that's how they've done it all year. They've been a resilient group all year and they showed that tonight. They executed really well and that's the bottom line."

In fact, with the possibility of a sweep, the Kings came out and had a strong first period. Trevor Lewis was stopped by goalie Mike Smith on a short-handed breakaway, and a few minutes later Smith stoned Mike Richards from in close during a delayed penalty.

Phoenix went on the power play 13 minutes into the first period and applied pressure to the Kings. Goalie Jonathan Quick tried to clear the puck along the glass, but the Coyotes managed to keep it in. The puck ended up in the corner on the stick of Shane Doan, who came out front and roofed a backhand to the far side before Quick could poke check him. The goal marked the first time the Kings' penalty killers had allowed a goal in 30 attempts. It was also a sensational play that showcased Doan's quick hands and scoring savvy; and it turned out to be a pivotal

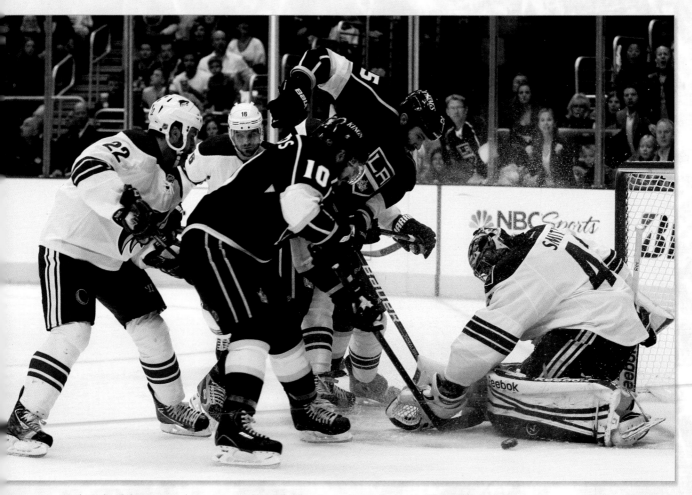

Mike Richards has a great chance to score, but Mike Smith is equal to the task in goal for the Coyotes.

Although the puck gets by Jonathan Quick, it rolls past the far post and out of harm's way.

play in the game, swinging the momentum in the Coyotes' favour.

Phoenix buckled down for the rest of the period and didn't allow that quick counterstrike the Kings had become famous for. The visitors went to the dressing room up a goal and continued their strong play in the middle period.

Doan scored again at 11:10 of the second period off a faceoff in the Los Angeles end. Antoine Vermette won it cleanly back to Doan at the top of

the circle. Doan's shot hit a camera inside the net and bounced out so quickly that play continued. At the next whistle, the referees went to video review, which confirmed that the puck had crossed the goal line.

The Kings pressed the rest of the game but couldn't beat Smith, who stopped 36 shots for a well-deserved shutout.

"I think I might have been caught up a little bit in trying to be overly physical in the other games, had

opportunities to play with the puck, make plays, take the puck to the net in the last couple games and didn't do it as well," Doan said. "It was brought to my attention by some people that's going to help you out with that. I think that was a big part of our game tonight. There were a few more times where we had pucks where we could try to get to the net."

Los Angeles was 0-for-6 with the man advantage, but the team had been doing so much so well through the playoffs thus far that a lapse was bound to happen at some point. The key was to bounce back.

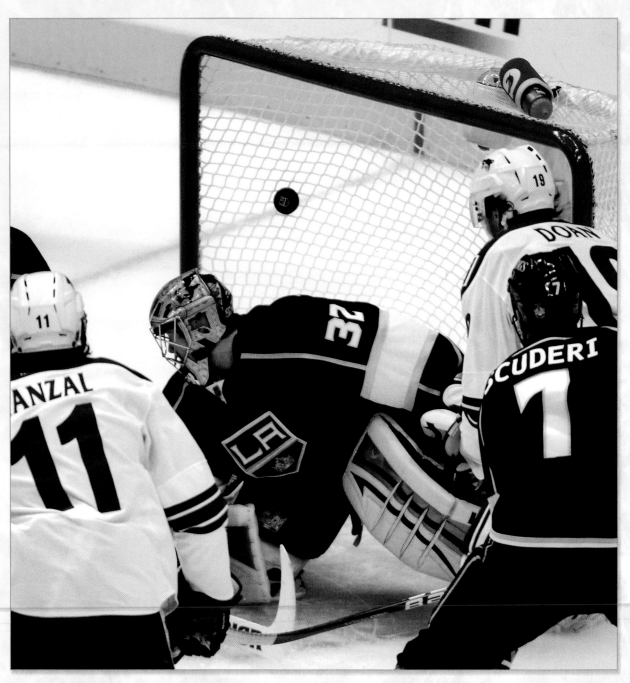

Shane Doan scores a power-play goal by coming out of the corner and tucking a backhand high to the far side.

GAME FIVE — *MAY 22, 2012*

Los Angeles 4 at Phoenix 3 (OT)

(Los Angeles wins series 4–1)

The Coyotes couldn't parlay their strong road performance in Game 4 into a home win three nights later, while the Kings continued their winning ways on the road for an eighth straight victory away from STAPLES Center. By the end of the night, the Kings had advanced to the Stanley Cup Final for the second time in franchise history – and the first time in 19 years – while the Cinderella Coyotes were heading home.

"I don't even know what to say," said defenceman Drew Doughty, who played a key role in the win. "We're just so happy in here. I'm so excited, but at the same time we're going to celebrate tonight and today and enjoy it. Tomorrow, we're right back at it and we're in the Stanley Cup [Final]. That's what we've dreamt of our whole lives and what we've worked for [since the] summer."

The Coyotes got their fans into it early with a power-play goal. Martin Hanzal was stationed at the top of the right faceoff circle and took a clean pass from Radim Vrbata before snapping a shot home to give Phoenix the lead. Taylor Pyatt tipped the shot on its way in and got credit for the goal.

But just when it seemed like Phoenix had gotten a foot in the door this series, the Kings made an emphatic statement to the contrary. Midway through the period, shorthanded, with a faceoff in the Coyotes end, the Kings tied the score. They won the draw and the puck came back to defenceman Drew Doughty. His shot was nicely tipped in front by Anze Kopitar.

Mike Richards scores in the second period to help the visiting Kings eliminate Phoenix in Game 5.

It's all over but the handshakes, as Phoenix's dream run ends while the Kings advance to the Cup Final for the first time since 1993.

The Coyotes took the lead again early in the second period when Marc-Antoine Pouliot got to a loose puck in the slot and beat Jonathan Quick with a shot. That lead wouldn't last long, however.

Just under five minutes later, Doughty continued to show his hockey smarts by taking the puck at the point along the boards, moving laterally along the blue line, and firing a simple snap shot through traffic that went all the way in. No big slap shot, no big wind up. Just find the lane and get the puck on net. That simple play led to the Kings' first goal of the game and now the second as well.

Two-and-a-half minutes later, the Kings took their first lead of the game. Dustin Penner drove hard down the right wing and cut in on goal, drawing players and creating havoc as he went. The puck came out front where Mike Richards got off a quick shot that beat the overwhelmed Smith, silencing the crowd and introducing the possibility of elimination into the game.

But the Coyotes answered quickly. Pyatt came down the left boards and passed in front, where Keith Yandle got his stick on the puck to beat Quick and tie the game, 3–3, at 16:23. The rest of regulation went without a goal, though not for a lack of chances. Midway through the third period, the Coyotes had a lengthy five-on-three situation but couldn't put the game away. As the final period progressed, it became clear that the next goal would win the game, but neither team scored and the game went to overtime.

Doughty took an interference penalty in the extra period, giving the home team hope, but Phoenix couldn't capitalize. The teams all knew what was on the line, but as it had all through the postseason, the Kings' effort was greater than their opponents.

On the winning play, Jeff Carter took the puck down the right wing on the rush, but his shot was stopped by Smith. The puck came right to Penner, and he backhanded it over Smith to give the Kings the game and series win.

"Things have come together at the right time for us," Brown said. "It is one of those things where we are getting contributions from everyone. We've had different heroes on different nights, and that goes a long way. It has a snowball effect, and you don't have to rely on the same guys each and every night."

STANLEY CUP FINAL 2012

LA · NHL · NJ DEVILS ™

GAME ONE — *May 30, 2012*

Los Angeles 2 at New Jersey 1 (OT)
(Los Angeles leads 1–0)

The Los Angeles Kings continued a record road run in the playoffs, defeating New Jersey 2–1 in overtime to go up 1–0 in the Stanley Cup Final. It was the Kings' ninth straight win away from the STAPLES Center in the 2012 playoffs, as well as their third straight OT win. The hero was none other than Anze Kopitar, the team's leading scorer of the last four years.

"It's just a big win, a big win in Game 1, and we focus now on Game 2 and try to win Game 2," said Jarret Stoll. "That's it. It doesn't matter if it's two in a row or 40 in a row on the road. The numbers don't really matter right now. It's whether or not we find a way to win."

A simple play inside the L.A. zone created the breakaway that won the game. It started when the Devils' Marek Zidlicky unwisely pinched in at the Kings blue line and was caught up ice. Justin Williams got the puck at centre and, as two Devils came to him, he made a great backhand pass to open ice in the middle where Kopitar collected the puck and went in alone. Kopitar then deked Martin Brodeur and stuffed the puck in the open side. The Kings' bench emptied in celebration at 8:13 of the fourth period.

New Jersey goalie Martin Brodeur lunges across the ice to sweep the puck out of harm's way.

64

Stanley Cup Final – Los Angeles Kings vs. New Jersey Devils

Stephen Gionta of New Jersey takes Jeff Carter into the boards and out of the play.

Stanley Cup Final – Los Angeles Kings vs. New Jersey Devils

65

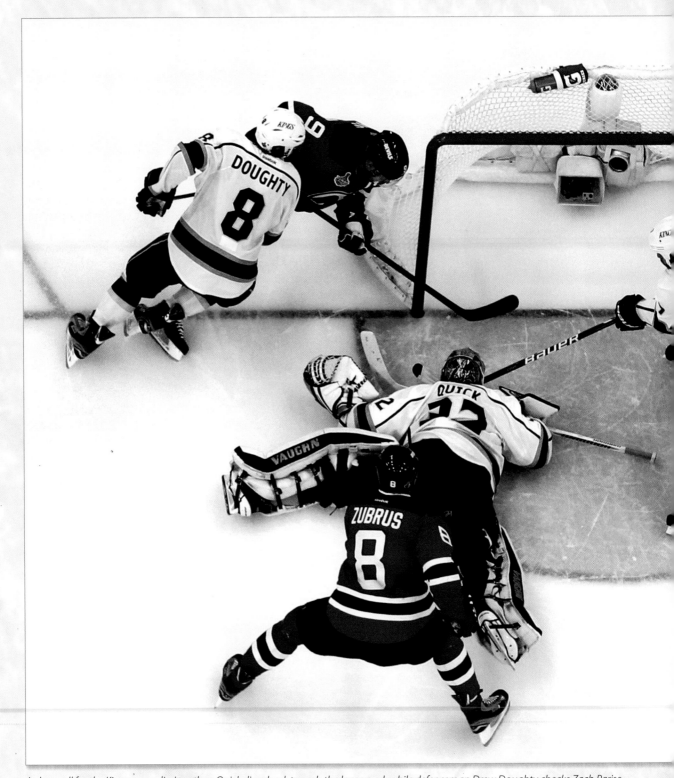

A close call for the Kings as goalie Jonathan Quick dives back to grab the loose puck while defenceman Drew Doughty checks Zach Parise.

"I didn't know if they had a backchecker coming, but I knew Kopi was in the area over there," Williams said. "That's when you just throw an area pass over there; hopefully he skates into it and hopefully it's timed right. Fortunately it was."

The Kings started strong and didn't allow the Devils to forecheck with their usual intensity or success. Indeed, it seemed like a game of wills, a clash of two styles of play, and on this night the Kings prevailed.

"The start wasn't good," said Ilya Kovalchuk of the Devils, their leading scorer in the first three rounds of the playoffs. "We tried to do some different things that we don't want to do and got out of our game plan a bit. We turned the puck over a lot. It's just one game. It's a long series, so we have to prepare as best as we can."

Colin Fraser got the only goal of the first period when he parked himself in front and snapped home a nice pass from Jordan Nolan behind the net through Brodeur's pads. Nolan had pressured Mark Fayne into turning the puck over after tenacious forechecking.

It looked like the Kings would control the game the rest of the way. They kept the Devils to the outside and didn't allow so much as a shot on goal for the first 14 minutes of the middle period, but the home side managed to tie the score with just 1:12 left. Anton Volchenkov was given credit for the goal, but his quick shot from the point actually went in off the shoulder of Slava Voynov.

Jonathan Quick, who faced only 17 shots in Game 1, didn't have to stop the most dangerous scoring chance of a tight-checking third period. The Devils' Fayne was perfectly positioned in the slot with Quick out of position when a bouncing puck landed right on the New Jersey player's stick. He had an empty net to shoot at, but the puck bounced high and rolled harmlessly into the corner as he tried to shoot.

"It's definitely tough knowing if one of those go in, then it would've been a win for us," Fayne admitted. "But it's also encouraging that we had those opportunities. We know if we keep playing hard, keep pressing then we'll get some of those bounces."

Stanley Cup Final – Los Angeles Kings vs. New Jersey Devils

67

GAME TWO — *June 2, 2012*

Los Angeles 2 at New Jersey 1 (OT)

(Los Angeles leads series 2–0)

The New Jersey Devils played better in Game 2 than they had in the series opener. In fact, in many ways, they were the better team. They got better goaltending, had more quality scoring chances, played with the full support of the hometown fans – but still they lost.

The hero for Los Angeles was Jeff Carter, who scored at 13:42 of overtime to give the Kings a commanding 2–0 series lead heading home for the next two games. He carried the puck inside the New Jersey end and fired a shot at Martin Brodeur, but the goalie kicked the puck away. Carter got the rebound, circled the net and came out front, and fired again.

This time his shot to the short side through traffic found its way to the back of the net, giving the Kings an NHL record 10th straight road win. The Kings were now 4–0 in OT in 2012 (all on the road) and, for the fourth time in as many series, they took a 2–0 lead on the road. They now were going home with a chance to win the Stanley Cup before their home fans.

"He's a goal-scorer," offered Kings coach Darryl Sutter of Carter. "You know what? You're counting on him to score a big goal."

Kings defenceman Drew Doughty celebrates his first-period goal, which stood as the only goal of the game until early in the third.

L.A.'s Jeff Carter closes in on goalie Martin Brodeur, who focuses on making the save.

Stanley Cup Final – Los Angeles Kings vs. New Jersey Devils

69

Drew Doughty gave L.A. a 1–0 lead just 7:49 into the game when he made a fine solo dash from one end of the ice to the other. He beat one man at centre ice, another at the Devils' blue line, and then snapped a wicked shot past the blocker of Brodeur.

"I just saw some ice in front of me, decided to skate with the puck," Doughty described. "I don't know who the defenceman was, but I tried to use him as a screen. Marty has that quick glove so I went blocker side. I didn't even know it went in actually, but luckily, it did."

That goal looked like it might stand up as the winner. The Kings used their superior size and speed the rest of the game to control play and limit New Jersey's offence. When the Devils did get an in-close chance, Jonathan Quick was there to make the save, just as he had done all playoffs.

New Jersey got the tying goal 2:59 into the third period when Marek Zidlicky's point shot was deflected in front by Ryan Carter, beating Quick to the far side. The home side outshot the Kings 30–12 through three periods, but L.A. remained poised and calm when under pressure. Carter's timely goal was just another in a series of heroic moments for the Kings in these playoffs.

"It's unfortunate, but with a little luck on our side, we could be up 2–0," Brodeur said. "I think we have to find that positive and go into L.A. and sneak one game as early as we can and go from there. It makes it a little harder, but we're here now."

"You don't win the Cup winning two games in the Final," the Kings' Jarret Stoll said philosophically. "We haven't won anything yet."

Jeff Carter's snap-shot from the high slot beats Martin Brodeur to the stick side in overtime to give the visiting Kings a 2–1 win and 2–0 series lead.

70

Stanley Cup Final – Los Angeles Kings vs. New Jersey Devils

Stanley Cup Final – Los Angeles Kings vs. New Jersey Devils

GAME THREE — June 4, 2012

New Jersey 0 at Los Angeles 4

(Los Angeles leads series 3–0)

Absolutely incredible. It seemed to be getting easier for Los Angeles as they advanced closer to their first Stanley Cup Championship. The Kings won for the third time in as many games against the Devils, becoming the first team in NHL history to go up 3–0 in all four rounds under the current, best-of-seven playoff format, which began in 1987. In Game 3, they did it with the help of their expected star – goalie Jonathan Quick – and an unexpected one – their power play.

Quick was excellent all night and spectacular when he needed to be, blocking all 22 shots for his third shutout of the playoffs. New Jersey had managed just two goals in three games, and the Kings have given up a mere 24 goals in 17 playoff games in 2012.

The Kings' power play, previously the only weak link in their game, scored twice in Game 3, and their penalty kill shut down the Devils during six short-handed situations through two periods, including a lengthy five-on-three in the first.

"We need to get that first goal out, absolutely," said New Jersey coach Peter DeBoer. "We had some power-play opportunities there. We need to score one . . . . Their goalie made some big saves early. We couldn't get one."

Alec Martinez got the first goal of the game early in the second when he banged in a loose puck from the side of Martin Brodeur's left pad. The goalie

Anze Kopitar (out of frame) scores the game's second goal as Justin Williams (foreground) and Dustin Brown celebrate.

Bodies converge around the crease of Martin Brodeur as the goalie calmly freezes the puck.

Stanley Cup Final – Los Angeles Kings vs. New Jersey Devils

73

protested that he had frozen the puck, but referee Dan O'Halloran ruled that it was in sight and allowed the score. From then on, the Kings dominated.

The Kings made it 2–0 at 15:07 of the second period on a gorgeous three-way passing play reminiscent of the 1980s Oilers. Justin Williams took the puck in down the right side and made a back pass off the boards to Dustin Brown, who fired a perfect pass across to Anze Kopitar. Kopitar had beaten Zach Parise and was roaring toward the goal. No sooner was the puck on Kopitar's stick than he drilled a one-timer over the sliding Broduer.

"[Williams] made the little bank behind and taking the hit," Brown described. "Their defenceman kind of overplayed that, and I had a little time. I didn't really see [Kopitar] beyond the guy, I just knew he was coming, and I just put it there. As good as the pass was, the shot was probably better."

In the third period, the Kings allowed no opportunity for a comeback. Jeff Carter and Williams scored man-advantage goals two and a half minutes apart to make it 4–0, and from there it was a matter of running down the clock to a 3–0 series lead.

"I think there will be added pressure because we are at home and the possibility of winning it at home is pretty enticing," offered Brown, trying to downplay his team's dominance thus far.

Defenceman Willie Mitchell was even more emphatic in the team's focus. "Coach [Darryl Sutter] says it best, 'You get nothing for three [wins].' That's why the fourth is the toughest one. We're going to enjoy it, and we're going to prepare just like we have the rest of this postseason for the next one. We're not naive to the situation. We're definitely not. You try and fuel that energy to motivate you for the next one."

And for the Kings, they sincerely hoped "the next one" and "the last one" meant the same thing.

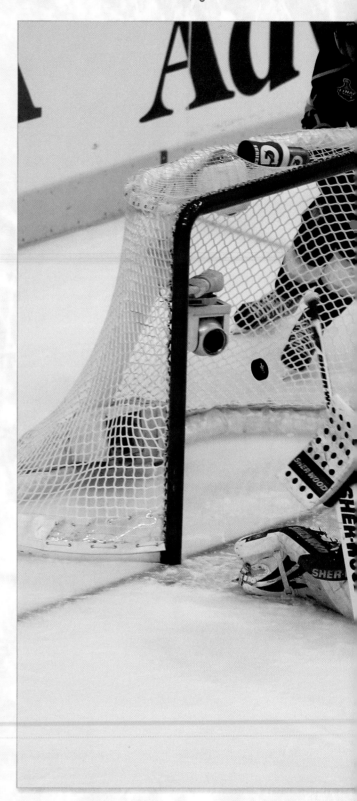

L.A.'s Justin Williams scores a third-period power-play goal to put Game 3 out of reach.

74

Stanley Cup Final – Los Angeles Kings vs. New Jersey Devils

Stanley Cup Final – Los Angeles Kings vs. New Jersey Devils

GAME FOUR — *June 6, 2012*

New Jersey 3 at Los Angeles 1

(Los Angeles leads series 3–1)

For the third time in four playoff series, the Los Angeles Kings failed to close a series on home ice. In Game 4, a scoreless first 40 minutes produced a tense third period in which the visiting New Jersey Devils skated to an impressive 3–1 victory.

"You know, I think we wanted to make them jump on a plane and come to New Jersey," suggested Devils' goalie Martin Brodeur. "We had to go anyway – might as well get a game over there. I think it's a tough situation, you know, for us to be in. We pulled it off, one game. We'll take it one game at a time. But I'm sure they're not happy to make that trip. We'll try to make it miserable for them again."

The first period was a close-checking chess match where both teams knew what was at stake. Referees called two minor penalties against each team, but there was only one real scoring chance on any of the power plays. That came in the dying seconds of the period when Anze Kopitar rang a low shot off the post.

The second period was more of the same. The Kings played better and had the only man-advantage of the frame, but the Devils hung in there and kept the game within reach. The forecheck and speed of the Kings was not as strong as it had been, but Jonathan Quick was so solid in goal it simply didn't look as though the Devils could get a puck past him.

The best chance of the second period came from Simon Gagne. Playing his second game after missing

Goalie Martin Brodeur maintains admirable calm as skaters crowd his crease from both sides.

76

Stanley Cup Final – Los Angeles Kings vs. New Jersey Devils

Drew Doughty's point shot on the power play tied the game for Los Angeles, 1–1, just 62 seconds after the Devils opened the scoring in the third period.

Stanley Cup Final – Los Angeles Kings vs. New Jersey Devils

77

the last half of the regular season and the first 16 games of the playoffs, he drove down the left wing and blasted a shot at Brodeur, who calmly made the save.

Early in the third period, the Kings had a sensational chance to get the first goal when Gagne intercepted a pass from Bryce Salvador at the Los Angeles blue line. Gagne couldn't get enough speed for a breakaway, so he made a great pass to Trevor Lewis, who went in alone. Brodeur made a huge save, not fooled by Lewis' deke.

The Devils ended up striking first midway through the final frame. Salvador pinched to keep the puck in the Los Angeles end, and Dainius Zubrus did some fine spade work down in the corner. He got the puck back to the point, and Quick made a save on Salvador's shot only to have Patrik Elias backhand the rebound into the open side.

Just as the Kings had done all postseason, they responded almost immediately. They got a power play less than a minute later thanks to a David Clarkson boarding penalty, and Drew Doughty's low point-shot just six seconds later went through several bodies and between Brodeur's pads.

The Devils got the go-ahead goal with less than five minutes to go thanks to a turnover at centre ice. Clarkson brought the puck in, found Adam Henrique on the far side, and Henrique buried a quick shot past the blocker of Quick to silence the crowd. It was Henrique's fourth goal of the playoffs, three of which were game-winners.

Ilya Kovalchuk got an empty netter to close out the scoring and force a fifth game in New Jersey three nights later.

"We couldn't score," Kopitar admitted. "We had a couple of chances, and we didn't bear down. We didn't get a couple of bounces in, and you have to create your own bounces. They played with a little more desperation than we did, and we have to correct that in Game 5."

Los Angeles captain Dustin Brown looks for a rebound in front of Martin Brodeur.

78

Stanley Cup Final – Los Angeles Kings vs. New Jersey Devils

GAME FIVE — *June 9, 2012*

Los Angeles 1 at **New Jersey 2**

(Los Angeles leads series 3–2)

The Kings suffered their first road loss of the 2012 Playoffs, while the Devils' 2–1 road win put them right back in the series and sent the Final back to California for Game 6. Timely goaltending and the ability to bury scoring chances was the difference in Game 5, with the Devils besting Los Angeles in both categories.

"Sure, there is anxiety," said Los Angeles forward Justin Williams. "We haven't lost two games in a row. We've played pretty hard. This is the Stanley Cup Final – it isn't supposed to be easy. This is a grind. They're a heck of a team over there with a lot of character and a lot of grit. They battled hard to keep that one-goal lead."

Both teams started the game looking to score, eschewing tight defensive play in favour of offense and creativity. The visiting Kings had the first great chance when Justin Williams beat goalie Martin Brodeur with a wrist shot, only to have the puck clang off the post. A short time later, Jonathan Quick allowed a point shot to skitter through his pads, but Drew Doughty cleared the puck out of harm's way.

Despite the Kings' chances, it was the Devils who scored first. On a power play midway through the first period Quick played the puck behind his own goal. He tried to angle a pass to a defenceman, but Zach Parise swooped in and wrapped the puck in before Quick could get back to his crease. It was the Devils' first power play goal of the Final.

Early in the second period, Williams tied things up for the Kings. He took the puck down the right side, cut to the middle in the New Jersey end, and continued unobstructed. He waited for traffic to clog the middle, and then drilled a great shot past Brodeur.

Moments later, Jarret Stoll had a breakaway with a chance to give the Kings the lead, but he was held up enough that he only managed a weak shot on Brodeur. That shot on goal increased the intensity of the game as the teams exchanged several scoring chances and big hits through the rest of the period.

The Devils went ahead midway through the second when a gentle point shot from Bryce Salvador bounced off Slava Voynov and into the net. It was the kind of improbable goal Quick never would have allowed when things were going right – and just the kind of goal that indicated things were going wrong.

80

Stanley Cup Final – Los Angeles Kings vs. New Jersey Devils

Zach Parise manages to stuff the puck in the short side before Jonathan Quick can cover the post.

tanley Cup Final – Los Angeles Kings vs. New Jersey Devils

81

The Kings' best chance to tie the game again came on a power play late in the second period. Doughty went around the net and passed to Williams, whose quick shot from the top of the crease was covered down low by Brodeur. The Devils went to the dressing room with a 2–1 lead after 40 minutes.

In the third period the Kings were unable to generate much offence against a Devils team that was more tenacious and quicker to the puck. The few chances they did get were stymied by Brodeur, who also had lady luck on his side. No fewer than four Kings shots rang off the post over the course of the game, any of which would have likely changed the outcome had they gone in.

"We're still alive, so we have a chance," Brodeur said. "It's a difficult thing to get yourself ready for games like that. Now it's been two in a row. It drains you a lot. It takes a lot out of you. But, it's worth it."

New Jersey played exceptional team defence in front of Martin Brodeur, limiting the Kings to a single goal for the second straight game.

82

tanley Cup Final – Los Angeles Kings vs. New Jersey Devils

Martin Brodeur makes a brilliant poke check on Dustin Brown, whose excellent scoring chance is thwarted in the process.

tanley Cup Final – Los Angeles Kings vs. New Jersey Devils

83

GAME SIX — *June 11, 2012*

New Jersey 1 at **Los Angeles 6**
(Los Angeles wins Stanley Cup 4–2)

The Los Angeles Kings reeled off three quick power-play goals in the first period to squash any historic comeback bid by New Jersey and win their first Stanley Cup in franchise history.

Midway through the period, Steve Bernier hammered Rob Scuderi into the boards from behind and drew a five-minute major and a game misconduct. On the ensuing power play, the Kings scored three times, claiming a huge 3–0 lead.

A minute into the extended power play, captain Dustin Brown tipped in a point shot from Drew Doughty. It was his first goal in 10 games. Less than two minutes later, Jeff Carter tipped the puck at the top of the crease and it beat Brodeur.

Trevor Lewis scored the third of the power play with only nine seconds left in Bernier's major. Lewis popped in a rebound after Brodeur stopped Dwight King's shot off a rush down the right side. The Kings connected on six power-play goals in 12 attempts against the Devils during the Final.

Jeff Carter made it 4–0 early in the second period when he drilled a shot in the slot past Brodeur, reigniting the crowd and dimming any hopes of the Devils making a comeback. It came at 1:30 and was his eighth of the playoffs. Brown drew the first assist with a nice pass from the corner, his third point of the night.

To make matters worse for the Devils, Bryce Salvador took a four-minute high-sticking penalty on Jordan Nolan a short time later to give the Kings even more momentum. The Kings kept the puck in the New Jersey end for almost the full duration of the penalty, but didn't score. By the time Salvador returned to the ice the game was half over and a Devils comeback was becoming less likely.

New Jersey got its lone goal late in the second when Adam Henrique netted a rebound off of a Petr Sykora shot at 18:47.

84

Stanley Cup Final – Los Angeles Kings vs. New Jersey Devils

The Kings score one of their three power-play goals in the first period en route to a 6–1 win.

Stanley Cup Final – Los Angeles Kings vs. New Jersey Devils

85

The Kings took that hope away with a tenacious penalty kill, leaving New Jersey now 1-for-18 in the series with the man advantage. They got another power play later in the third period, but Marek Zidlicky negated that with a tripping penalty.

The Kings finished the night off in style. As the Devils pressed for a goal, Brodeur came to the bench with more than four minutes left, but on a delayed penalty Lewis got his second of the night with an empty netter. Just 15 seconds later, Brodeur back in, Matt Greene made it 6–1.

The celebrations began and, when the buzzer sounded, the Kings had gone from eighth place to Stanley Cup champions in a matter of two months.

Pandemonium ensues at the final buzzer as the Kings win the Stanley Cup!

Captain Justin Brown parades the Cup around ice as his teammates watch in awe.

Stanley Cup Final – Los Angeles Kings vs. New Jersey Devils

87

Drew Doughty hoists the Cup during the on-ice celebrations.

Bearded and soaking wet, the Kings enjoy some champagne out of the Cup in their dressing room.

Stanley Cup Final – Los Angeles Kings vs. New Jersey Devils

89

2012 Conn Smythe Trophy: *Jonathan Quick*

In the end, could it have been anyone else? A hockey team's success starts and finishes with the goalie, and there was little doubt during the 2012 Playoffs that without Jonathan Quick, the Los Angeles Kings couldn't have won the Stanley Cup.

Consider that Quick went head-to-head with Roberto Luongo of Vancouver in the first round and came out a winner. He faced down Brian Elliott of St. Louis. He went up against the Coyotes' Mike Smith, the hottest goalie in the league during the last part of the regular season, and won. And then, in his greatest challenge, he bested Martin Brodeur, the most successful goalie in NHL history, in a tense, six-game Final.

Quick was the backbone of the Kings' run to the Cup. His calm demeanour, his key saves, and his confidence all allowed the rest of the team to relax, knowing they could make a mistake and not lose the game. Quick could keep them in there.

His rise to the top has been incredible. He was the third goalie for the United States at the 2010 Olympics, but has since developed into a world-class puckstopper. The 26-year-old is the key to the long-term success of the Kings who hope to build on the success of their 2012 Cup win and return to the Final again in the coming years.

Goalie Jonathan Quick accepts the Conn Smythe Trophy from NHL commissioner Gary Bettman.

The Los Angeles Kings had never come close to the Stanley Cup before 1993. That year, an L.A. team led by Wayne Gretzky, who was at the height of his powers, stormed through the Campbell (now Western) Conference en route to its first Stanley Cup Final appearance in franchise history.

Gretzky had been acquired from the Edmonton Oilers on August 8, 1988, in the biggest trade in the history of hockey – arguably in all of sports history. The complex deal saw the Kings acquire No. 99 and two teammates, Mike Krushelnyski and Marty McSorley, for Jimmy Carson, Martin Gelinas, and first-round draft choices in 1989, 1991, and 1993 – as well as a whopping $15 million in cash.

The Kings got their money's worth, and then some. Gretzky's first years with the team brought new fan interest and success on the ice to go with it. In 1992–93, though, the season started off with worry as Gretzky played only 45 games, missing the first half of the year with a back injury. But far from being a setback, the injury ensured, Gretzky was more well-rested than he had ever been to start the playoffs.

The Kings opened the Campbell Conference Quarterfinals against the Calgary Flames, a series L.A. won in six games – a goalfest in which the Kings outscored the Flames 33–28. The Kings scored a whopping nine goals in each of their last two games to turn a 2–2 series in their favour.

The next round was a West Coast battle versus the Vancouver Canucks, and again the Kings needed six games to eliminate their rivals. Knotted 2–2 after four games, the Kings picked up close wins of 4–3 (on the road) and 5–3 (at home).

Then came the Conference Finals, this time a cross-continent affair with the Toronto Maple Leafs. The Leafs, led by diminutive captain Doug Gilmour, were having a sensational and surprising playoff run of their own. But Gretzky, a native Ontarian, always loved playing at Maple Leaf Gardens in front of his friends and family, and against the team he knew well from his childhood.

After a hard-fought start to the series, the Leafs went to California for Game 6 leading 3–2, with a chance to advance to the Final for the first time since 1967. Gretzky scored in overtime to force Game 7 in Toronto. In that game, spurred by the negative press he had been receiving, the Great One scored three goals and led the Kings to a 5–4 win, a game that he later called the most satisfying of his NHL career.

But the Kings, after 19 games in the first three rounds, had to travel coast to coast again, this time to face the Montreal Canadiens. The Habs had played only 15 games and were fresher, a fact that became the key of the series. The Kings, riding on the emotional high of their Game 7 win in Toronto, travelled a bit northeast to beat Montreal, 4–1, in the Cup Final opener, but ran out of gas after that. The Habs won the next four in a row to clinch their 24th, and most recent, Stanley Cup.

The Kings were never close to competing for the Cup again until the spring of 2012, some 19 years later. But for fans of the team, the wait has been worth it.

The Los Angeles Kings played in the Stanley Cup Final only once before the 2011–12 season, a 4–1 series loss to the Montreal Canadiens in 1993.

It was a game so remarkable, so incredible, that it was given a nickname: "The Miracle on Manchester." In the spring of 1982, the Los Angeles Kings and Edmonton Oilers played an opening-round, best-of-five playoff series. The Oilers held home-ice advantage with their 111 points, a whopping 48 ahead of the Kings in the Smythe Division standings.

The Oilers were just entering their prime, though they hadn't yet won a Stanley Cup. Still, they had the most explosive offensive team in League history, led by Wayne Gretzky, Mark Messier, and Paul Coffey.

Game 1 of the series set a record for goals scored in the playoffs, as the visiting Kings won, 10–8. Game 2 saw Gretzky score the overtime winner to give the Oilers a 3–2 win and tie the series. That set the stage for Game 3 in Los Angeles on April 10, 1982.

The Oilers started off like gangbusters, opening a 3–0 lead early in the second period and scoring two shorthanded goals on the same L.A. power play. By the end of the second, the Oilers had built a 5–0 lead and were on their way to a lopsided laugher.

But Jay Wells made it 5–1 at 2:46 of the third with the Kings' first goal of the game, and three minutes later Doug Smith scored on a power play to make it 5–2. A short time later, Charlie Simmer made it 5–3 on a lucky play in which Oilers' goalie Grant Fuhr and defenceman Randy Gregg fouled up, knocking the puck into their own goal. Now the game became interesting.

With only a few minutes left in the period and the teams playing four a side, Mark Hardy surprised Fuhr with a shot and it was 5–4. The Kings then had a late power play, but another error led to a short-handed breakaway by Oiler Pat Hughes, who was stopped cold by Kings' goaltender Mario Lessard.

In the final minute, with the Kings on the power play and Lessard on the bench for an extra attacker, L.A. pressed for the tying goal. It came when Steve Bozek got to a loose puck and lifted it over a sprawling Fuhr with just five seconds remaining in regulation.

Stunned, the Oilers went to the dressing room to prepare for overtime of a game they led 5–0 just 20 minutes before. Things only got worse in the fourth period. Just 2:35 in, Daryl Evans ripped a shot that blew past Fuhr to give Los Angeles a 6–5 win in the greatest comeback of the Stanley Cup playoffs.

The Fabulous Forum, as the Kings' arena was nicknamed, was situated on Manchester Boulevard,

and that game has since been called "The Miracle on Manchester." The Kings lost Game 4 at home, 3–2, but pulled off an incredible upset by beating the Oilers in Game 5, 7–4. It was one of the greatest upsets in playoff history, spurred by the greatest comeback.

Daryl Evans was the overtime hero for the Kings in the greatest comeback in Stanley Cup Playoff history.

On August 9, 1988, hockey changed forever. That was the day Wayne Gretzky was traded from the Edmonton Oilers to the Los Angeles Kings and the term "untouchable" was removed from hockey's lexicon. In many ways that day also heralded the birth of a new era for the NHL. By the time he left the Kings nearly a decade later, the League had expanded and the sport had grown from one of regional interest to one played and followed all over the United States.

In 1988 though, Gretzky arrived in a Los Angeles that had little interest in hockey. California was a part of the world that hadn't yet embraced the sport in the way they had the baseball or basketball. The fanfare that Gretzky brought with him translated to on-ice success for the Kings and soon, the team was setting attendance records at home and on the road.

At first blush, the most incredible aspect of the trade was that it didn't have any effect on Gretzky's performance on the ice. One would think that without teammates like Mark Messier, Jari Kurri, Paul Coffey, and Glenn Anderson, that Gretzky's offensive output would suffer. It didn't. He had 168 points in 78 games the year of the trade, second only to Mario Lemieux. Instead of those great Oilers as teammates, members of the Kings benefited by having The Great One as a linemate. Bernie Nicholls had a career-high 150 points and newcomer Luc Robitaille had 98. Gretzky kept his streak of Art Ross Trophy wins going over the next two years, but more incredibly, no other Kings player was in the top-10 in scoring. Without a strong supporting cast, Gretzky still flourished.

In the playoffs, the Kings knocked off the Oilers in 1989 and then lost to them in 1990, but Gretzky had his greatest impact in 1992–93 at a time when things looked they were at their nadir. He missed half a season with a back injury, but when he returned he was rested and able to take the Kings on a magical run to the Stanley Cup Final.

The Kings beat Toronto in Game 7 of the Conference Final, advancing to the Cup Final for the first time in franchise history. The Kings won Game 1 against Montreal 4–1, but the Habs were on a magical run of their own. They had won seven straight overtime games heading into the Final, and had three more wins in the extra frame against Los Angeles. They closed out the series in regulation with a 4–1 win.

While in Los Angeles Gretzky established records for most career goals as well as points, surpassing Gordie Howe in both categories. He brought a glitz and glamour to the Fabulous Forum commensurate with the NFL, MLB, and NBA. Stars came to see him play; kids started to wear Kings' No. 99 sweaters around town; hockey became Southern Cal cool in a way it never had before. As a result of his popularity, the League was able to expand to Anaheim and San Jose and along the southern U.S. states in a way that might not have been possible had Gretzky not been traded to the Kings.

His tenure with the King ended in 1996 when he was traded to St. Louis, but Gretzky continued to live in the Los Angeles area. As soon as the Kings made the 2012 Cup Final, he assured anyone who asked that he'd be at the STAPLES Center for Game 3, the first Kings home game in the series. Not only was he there; he dropped the ceremonial first puck after receiving a thunderous ovation. Gretzky was back on Kings' ice – and so was the Cup Final.

Wayne Gretzky gets ready to drop the puck prior to Game 3 at the STAPLES Center, June 4, 2012.

Wayne Gretzky became the all-time leading scorer with this goal against Vancouver on March 23, 1994, beating goalie Kirk McLean for his 802nd career goal, one more than Gordie Howe.

YEAR–BY–YEAR RECORD

	GP	W	L	T	OL	GF	GA	Pts
1967–68	74	31	33	10	—	200	224	72
1968–69	76	24	42	10	—	185	260	58
1969–70	76	14	52	10	—	168	290	38
1970–71	78	25	40	13	—	239	303	63
1971–72	78	20	49	9	—	206	305	49
1972–73	78	31	36	11	—	232	245	73
1973–74	78	33	33	12	—	233	231	78
1974–75	80	42	17	21	—	269	185	105
1975–76	80	38	33	9	—	263	265	85
1976–77	80	34	31	15	—	271	241	83
1977–78	80	31	34	15	—	243	245	77
1978–79	80	34	34	12	—	292	286	80
1979–80	80	30	36	14	—	290	313	74
1980–81	80	43	24	13	—	337	290	99
1981–82	80	24	41	15	—	314	369	63
1982–83	80	27	41	12	—	308	365	66
1983–84	80	23	44	13	—	309	376	59
1984–85	80	34	32	14	—	339	326	82
1985–86	80	23	49	8	—	284	389	54
1986–87	80	31	41	8	—	318	341	70
1987–88	80	30	42	8	—	318	359	68
1988–89	80	42	31	7	—	376	335	91
1989–90	80	34	39	7	—	338	337	75
1990–91	80	46	24	10	—	340	254	102
1991–92	80	35	31	14	—	287	296	84
1992–93	84	39	35	10	—	338	340	88
1993–94	84	27	45	12	—	294	322	66
1994–95	48	16	23	9	—	142	174	41
1995–96	82	24	40	18	—	256	302	66
1996–97	82	28	43	11	—	214	268	67
1997–98	82	38	33	11	—	227	225	87
1998–99	82	32	45	5	—	189	222	69
1999–2000	82	39	27	12	4	245	228	94
2000–01	82	38	28	13	3	252	228	92
2001–02	82	40	27	11	4	214	190	95
2002–03	82	33	37	6	6	203	221	78
2003–04	82	28	29	16	9	205	217	81
2004–05				No Season				
2005–06	82	42	35	—	5	249	270	89
2006–07	82	27	41	—	14	227	283	68
2007–08	82	32	43	—	7	231	266	71
2008–09	82	34	37	—	11	207	234	79
2009–10	82	46	27	—	9	241	219	101
2010–11	82	46	30	—	6	219	198	98
2011–12	82	40	27	—	15	194	179	95

1968

QUARTERFINALS

April 4	Minnesota 1 at Los Angeles 2
April 6	Minnesota 0 at Los Angeles 2
April 9	Los Angeles 5 at Minnesota 7
April 11	Los Angeles 2 at Minnesota 3
April 13	Minnesota 2 at Los Angeles 3
April 16	Los Angeles 3 at Minnesota 4 (OT)
April 18	Minnesota 9 at Los Angeles 4

Minnesota wins best-of-seven 4–3

1969

QUARTERFINALS

April 2	Los Angeles 5 at Oakland 4 (OT)
April 3	Los Angeles 2 at Oakland 4
April 5	Oakland 5 at Los Angeles 2
April 6	Oakland 2 at Los Angeles 4
April 9	Los Angeles 1 at Oakland 4
April 10	Oakland 3 at Los Angeles 4
April 13	Los Angeles 5 at Oakland 3

Los Angeles wins best-of-seven 4–3

SEMI-FINALS

April 15	Los Angeles 0 at St. Louis 4
April 17	Los Angeles 2 at St. Louis 3
April 19	St. Louis 5 at Los Angeles 2
April 20	St. Louis 4 at Los Angeles 1

St. Louis wins best-of-seven 4–0

1974

QUARTERFINALS

April 10	Kings 1 at Chicago 3
April 11	Kings 1 at Chicago 4
April 13	Chicago 1 at Los Angeles 0
April 14	Chicago 1 at Los Angeles 5
April 16	Los Angeles 0 at Chicago 1

Chicago wins best-of-seven 4–1

1975

PRELIMINARY ROUND

April 8	Toronto 2 at Los Angeles 3 (OT)
April 10	Los Angeles 2 at Toronto 3 (OT)
April 11	Toronto 2 at Los Angeles 1

Toronto wins best-of-three 2–1

1976

PRELIMINARY ROUND

| April 6 | Atlanta 1 at Los Angeles 2 |
| April 8 | Los Angeles 1 at Atlanta 0 |

Los Angeles wins best-of-three 2–0

QUARTERFINALS

April 11	Los Angeles 0 at Boston 4
April 13	Los Angeles 3 at Boston 2 (OT)
April 15	Boston 4 at Los Angeles 6
April 17	Boston 3 at Los Angeles 0
April 20	Los Angeles 1 at Boston 7
April 22	Boston 3 at Los Angeles 4 (OT)
April 25	Los Angeles 0 at Boston 3

Boston wins best-of-seven 4–3

1977

PRELIMINARY ROUND

April 5	Atlanta 2 at Los Angeles 5
April 7	Los Angeles 2 at Atlanta 3
April 9	Atlanta 2 at Los Angeles 4

Los Angeles wins best-of-three 2–1

QUARTERFINALS

April 11	Los Angeles 3 at Boston 8
April 13	Los Angeles 2 at Boston 6
April 15	Boston 7 at Los Angeles 6
April 17	Boston 4 at Los Angeles 7
April 19	Los Angeles 3 at Boston 1
April 21	Boston 4 at Los Angeles 3

Boston wins best-of-seven 4–2

1978

PRELIMINARY ROUND

| April 11 | Los Angeles 3 at Toronto 7 |
| April 13 | Toronto 4 at Los Angeles 0 |

Toronto wins best-of-three 2–0

1979

PRELIMINARY ROUND

| April 10 | NY Rangers 7 at Los Angeles 1 |
| April 12 | NY Rangers 2 at Los Angeles 1 (OT) |

Rangers win best-of-three 2–0

1980

PRELIMINARY ROUND

April 8	Los Angeles 1 at NY Islanders 8
April 9	Los Angeles 6 at NY Islanders 3
April 11	NY Islanders 4 at Los Angeles 3 (OT)
April 12	NY Islanders 6 at Los Angeles 0

Islanders win best-of-five 3–1

1981

PRELIMINARY ROUND

April 8	NY Rangers 3 at Los Angeles 1
April 9	NY Rangers 4 at Los Angeles 5
April 11	Los Angeles 3 at NY Rangers 10
April 12	Los Angeles 3 at NY Rangers 6

Rangers win best-of-five 3–1

1982

DIVISION SEMIFINALS

April 7	Los Angeles 10 at Edmonton 8
April 8	Los Angeles 2 at Edmonton 3 (OT)
April 10	Edmonton 5 at Los Angeles 6 (OT)
April 12	Edmonton 3 at Los Angeles 2
April 13	Los Angeles 7 at Edmonton 4

Los Angeles wins best-of-five 3–2

DIVISION FINALS

April 15	Los Angeles 2 at Vancouver 3
April 16	Los Angeles 3 at Vancouver 2 (OT)
April 18	Vancouver 4 at Los Angeles 3 (OT)
April 19	Vancouver 5 at Los Angeles 4
April 21	Los Angeles 2 at Vancouver 5

Vancouver wins best-of-seven 4–1

1985

DIVISION SEMIFINALS

April 10	Los Angeles 2 at Edmonton 3 (OT)
April 11	Los Angeles 2 at Edmonton 4
April 13	Edmonton 4 at Los Angeles 3 (OT)

Edmonton wins best-of-five 3–0

1987

DIVISION SEMIFINALS

April 8	Los Angeles 5 at Edmonton 2
April 9	Los Angeles 3 at Edmonton 13
April 11	Edmonton 6 at Los Angeles 5
April 12	Edmonton 6 at Los Angeles 3
April 14	Los Angeles 4 at Edmonton 5

Edmonton wins best-of-seven 4–1

1988

DIVISION SEMIFINALS

April 6	Los Angeles 2 at Calgary 9
April 7	Los Angeles 4 at Calgary 6
April 9	Calgary 2 at Los Angeles 5
April 10	Calgary 7 at Los Angeles 3
April 12	Los Angeles 4 at Calgary 6

Calgary wins best-of-seven 4–1

1989

DIVISION SEMIFINALS

April 5	Edmonton 4 at Los Angeles 3
April 6	Edmonton 2 at Los Angeles 5
April 8	Los Angeles 0 at Edmonton 4
April 9	Los Angeles 3 at Edmonton 4
April 11	Edmonton 2 at Los Angeles 4
April 13	Los Angeles 4 at Edmonton 1
April 15	Edmonton 3 at Los Angeles 6

Los Angeles wins best-of-seven 4–3

DIVISION FINALS

April 18	Los Angeles 3 at Calgary 4 (OT)
April 20	Los Angeles 3 at Calgary 8
April 22	Calgary 5 at Los Angeles 2
April 24	Calgary 5 at Los Angeles 3

Calgary wins best-of-seven 4–0

1990

DIVISION SEMIFINALS

April 4	Los Angeles 5 at Calgary 3
April 6	Los Angeles 5 at Calgary 8
April 8	Calgary 1 at Los Angeles 2 (OT)
April 10	Calgary 4 at Los Angeles 12
April 12	Los Angeles 1 at Calgary 5
April 14	Calgary 3 at Los Angeles 4 (2OT)

Los Angeles wins best-of-seven 4–2

DIVISION FINALS

April 18	Los Angeles 0 at Edmonton 7
April 20	Los Angeles 1 at Edmonton 6
April 22	Edmonton 5 at Los Angeles 4
April 24	Edmonton 6 at Los Angeles 5 (OT)

Edmonton wins best-of-seven 4–0

1991

DIVISION SEMIFINALS

April 4	Vancouver 6 at Los Angeles 5
April 6	Vancouver 2 at Los Angeles 3 (OT)
April 8	Los Angeles 1 at Vancouver 2 (OT)
April 10	Los Angeles 6 at Vancouver 1
April 12	Vancouver 4 at Los Angeles 7
April 14	Los Angeles 4 at Vancouver 1

Los Angeles wins best-of-seven 4–2

DIVISION FINALS

April 18	Edmonton 3 at Los Angeles 4 (OT)
April 20	Edmonton 4 at Los Angeles 3 (2OT)
April 22	Los Angeles 3 at Edmonton 4 (2OT)
April 24	Los Angeles 2 at Edmonton 4
April 26	Edmonton 2 at Los Angeles 5
April 28	Los Angeles 3 at Edmonton 4 (OT)

Edmonton wins best-of-seven 4–2

1992

DIVISION SEMIFINALS

April 18	Edmonton 3 at Los Angeles 1
April 20	Edmonton 5 at Los Angeles 8
April 22	Los Angeles 3 at Edmonton 4
April 24	Los Angeles 4 at Edmonton 3
April 26	Edmonton 5 at Los Angeles 2
April 28	Los Angeles 0 at Edmonton 3

Edmonton wins best-of-seven 4–2

1993

DIVISION SEMIFINALS

April 18	Los Angeles 6 at Calgary 3
April 21	Los Angeles 4 at Calgary 9
April 23	Calgary 5 at Los Angeles 2
April 25	Calgary 1 at Los Angeles 3
April 27	Los Angeles 9 at Calgary 4
April 29	Calgary 6 at Los Angeles 9

Los Angeles wins best-of-seven 4–2

DIVISION FINALS

May 2	Los Angeles 2 at Vancouver 5
May 5	Los Angeles 6 at Vancouver 3
May 7	Vancouver 4 at Los Angeles 7
May 9	Vancouver 7 at Los Angeles 2
May 11	Los Angeles 4 at Vancouver 3 (2OT)
May 13	Vancouver 3 at Los Angeles 5

Los Angeles wins best-of-seven 4–2

CONFERENCE FINALS

May 17	Los Angeles 1 at Toronto 4
May 19	Los Angeles 3 at Toronto 2
May 21	Toronto 2 at Los Angeles 4
May 23	Toronto 4 at Los Angeles 2
May 25	Los Angeles 2 at Toronto 3 (OT)
May 27	Toronto 4 at Los Angeles 5 (OT)
May 29	Los Angeles 5 at Toronto 4

Los Angeles wins best-of-seven 4–3

STANLEY CUP FINALS

June 1	Los Angeles 4 at Montreal 1
June 3	Los Angeles 2 at Montreal 3 (OT)
June 5	Montreal 4 at Los Angeles 3 (OT)
June 7	Montreal 3 at Los Angeles 2 (OT)
June 9	Los Angeles 1 at Montreal 4

Montreal wins best-of-seven 4–1

1998

CONFERENCE QUARTERFINALS

April 23	Los Angeles 3 at St. Louis 8
April 25	Los Angeles 1 at St. Louis 2
April 27	St. Louis 4 at Los Angeles 3
April 30	St. Louis 2 at Los Angeles 1

St. Louis wins best-of-seven 4–0

2000

CONFERENCE QUARTERFINALS

April 13	Los Angeles 0 at Detroit 2
April 15	Los Angeles 5 at Detroit 8
April 17	Detroit 2 at Los Angeles 1
April 19	Detroit 3 at Los Angeles 0

Detroit wins best-of-seven 4–0

2001

CONFERENCE QUARTERFINALS

April 11	Los Angeles 3 at Detroit 5
April 14	Los Angeles 0 at Detroit 4
April 15	Detroit 1 at Los Angeles 2
April 18	Detroit 3 at Los Angeles 4 (OT)
April 21	Los Angeles 3 at Detroit 2
April 23	Detroit 2 at Los Angeles 3 (OT)

Los Angeles wins best-of-seven 4–2

CONFERENCE SEMIFINALS

April 26	Los Angeles 4 at Colorado 3 (OT)
April 28	Los Angeles 0 at Colorado 2
April 30	Colorado 4 at Los Angeles 3
May 2	Colorado 3 at Los Angeles 0
May 4	Los Angeles 1 at Colorado 0
May 6	Colorado 0 at Los Angeles 1 (2OT)
May 9	Los Angeles 1 at Colorado 5

Colorado wins best-of-seven 4–3

2002

CONFERENCE QUARTERFINALS

April 18	Los Angeles 3 at Colorado 4
April 20	Los Angeles 3 at Colorado 5
April 22	Colorado 1 at Los Angeles 3
April 23	Colorado 1 at Los Angeles 0
April 25	Los Angeles 1 at Colorado 0 (OT)
April 27	Colorado 1 at Los Angeles 3
April 29	Los Angeles 0 at Colorado 4

Colorado wins best-of-seven 4–3

2010

CONFERENCE QUARTERFINALS

April 15	Los Angeles 2 at Vancouver 3 (OT)
April 17	Los Angeles 3 at Vancouver 2 (OT)
April 19	Vancouver 3 at Los Angeles 5
April 21	Vancouver 6 at Los Angeles 4
April 23	Los Angeles 2 at Vancouver 7
April 25	Vancouver 4 at Los Angeles 2

Vancouver wins best-of-seven 4–2

2011

CONFERENCE QUARTERFINALS

April 14	Los Angeles 2 at San Jose 3 (OT)
April 16	Los Angeles 4 at San Jose 0
April 17	San Jose 6 at Los Angeles 5 (OT)
April 21	San Jose 6 at Los Angeles 3
April 23	Los Angeles 3 San Jose 1
April 25	San Jose 4 at Los Angeles 3 (OT)

San Jose wins best-of-seven 4–2

Year	Team	Position	Player
1974–75	Second	Goalie	**Rogie Vachon**
1976–77	Second	Goalie	**Rogie Vachon**
1976–77	First	Centre	**Marcel Dionne**
1978–79	Second	Centre	**Marcel Dionne**
1979–80	First	Centre	**Marcel Dionne**
1979–80	First	Left Wing	**Charlie Simmer**
1980–81	First	Left Wing	**Charlie Simmer**
1980–81	Second	Centre	**Marcel Dionne**
1980–81	Second	Goalie	**Mario Lessard**
1980–81	Second	Right Wing	**Dave Taylor**
1986–87	Second	Left Wing	**Luc Robitaille**
1987–88	First	Left Wing	**Luc Robitaille**
1988–89	Second	Centre	**Wayne Gretzky**
1988–89	First	Left Wing	**Luc Robitaille**
1989–90	Second	Centre	**Wayne Gretzky**
1989–90	First	Left Wing	**Luc Robitaille**
1990–91	First	Centre	**Wayne Gretzky**
1990–91	First	Left Wing	**Luc Robitaille**
1991–92	Second	Left Wing	**Luc Robitaille**
1992–93	First	Left Wing	**Luc Robitaille**
1993–94	Second	Centre	**Wayne Gretzky**
1997–98	First	Defence	**Rob Blake**
1999–2000	Second	Defence	**Rob Blake**
2000–01	Second	Left Wing	**Luc Robitaille**

KINGS IN THE HOCKEY HALL OF FAME

Player	Induction Year	Years with Kings
Paul Coffey	2004	1991–93
Marcel Dionne	1992	1974–87
Dick Duff	2006	1969–71
Grant Fuhr	2003	1994–95
Wayne Gretzky	1999	1988–96
Harry Howell	1979	1970–73
Red Kelly	1969	1967–69 (Coach)
Brian Kilrea	2003	1967–68
Jari Kurri	2001	1991–96
Jake Milford	1984	1973–77 (GM)
Larry Murphy	2004	1980–84
Roger Neilson	2002	1984 (Coach)
Bob Pulford	1991	1970–72; 1972–77 (Coach)
Larry Robinson	1995	1989–92; 1995–99 (Coach)
Luc Robitaille	2009	1986–94; 1997–2001; 2003–06
Terry Sawchuk	1971	1967–68
Steve Shutt	1993	1984–85
Billy Smith	1993	1971–72

30   **Rogie Vachon**   number retired February 14, 1985

16   **Marcel Dionne**   number retired November 8, 1990

18   **Dave Taylor**   number retired April 3, 1995

99   **Wayne Gretzky**   number retired October 9, 2002

20   **Luc Robitaille**   number retired January 20, 2007

Luc Robitaille is the most recent member of the Kings to have his number retired by the team.

Hart Memorial Trophy

Wayne Gretzky: 1988–89

Art Ross Trophy

Marcel Dionne: 1979–80
Wayne Gretzky: 1989–90
Wayne Gretzky: 1990–91
Wayne Gretzky: 1993–94

James Norris Memorial Trophy

Rob Blake: 1997–98

Calder Memorial Trophy

Luc Robitaille: 1986–87

Lady Byng Memorial Trophy

Marcel Dionne: 1976–77
Butch Goring: 1977–78
Wayne Gretzky: 1990–91
Wayne Gretzky: 1991–92
Wayne Gretzky: 1993–94

Defenceman Rob Blake won the Norris Trophy with the Kings in 1997–98.

Bill Masterton Memorial Trophy

Butch Goring: 1977–78
Bob Bourne: 1987–88
Dave Taylor: 1990–91

King Clancy Memorial Trophy

Dave Taylor: 1990–91

Jack Adams Award

Bob Pulford: 1974–75

Lester B. Pearson Award

Marcel Dionne: 1978–79
Marcel Dionne: 1979–80

NHL Foundation Player Award

Dustin Brown: 2010–11

2011

49	Christopher Gibson
80	Andy Andreoff
82	Nick Shore
110	Michael Mersch
140	Joel Lowry
200	Michael Schumacher

2010

15	Derek Forbort
47	Tyler Toffoli
70	Jordan Weal
148	Kevin Gravel
158	Maxim Kitsyn

2009

5	Brayden Schenn
35	Kyle Clifford
84	Nicolas Deslauriers
95	Jean-Francois Berube
96	Linden Vey
126	David Kolomatis
156	Michael Pelech
179	Brandon Kozun
186	Jordan Nolan
198	Nic Dowd

2008

2	Drew Doughty
13	Colten Teubert
32	Vyacheslav Voynov
63	Robert Czarnik
74	Andrew Campbell
88	Geordie Wudrick
123	Andrei Loktionov
153	Justin Azevedo
183	Garrett Roe

2007

4	Thomas Hickey
52	Oscar Moller
61	Wayne Simmonds
82	Bryan Cameron
95	Alec Martinez
109	Dwight King
124	Linden Rowat
137	Joshua Turnbull

184	Josh Kidd
188	Matt Fillier

2006

11	Jonathan Bernier
17	Trevor Lewis
48	Joey Ryan
74	Jeff Zatkoff
86	Bud Holloway
114	Niclas Andersen
134	David Meckler
144	Martin Nolet
164	Constantin Braun

2005

11	Anze Kopitar
50	Dany Roussin
60	T.J. Fast
72	Jonathan Quick
139	Patrik Hersley
184	Ryan McGinnis
206	Josh Meyers
226	John Seymour

2004

11	Lauri Tukonen
95	Paul Baier
110	Ned Lukacevic
143	Eric Neilson
174	Scott Parse
205	Mike Curry
221	Daniel Taylor
238	Yutaka Fukufuji
264	Valtteri Tenkanen

2003

13	Dustin Brown
26	Brian Boyle
27	Jeff Tambellini
44	Konstantin Pushkarev
82	Ryan Munce
152	Brady Murray
174	Esa Pirnes
231	Matt Zaba
244	Mike Sullivan
274	Martin Guerin

2002

18	Denis Grebeshkov
50	Sergei Anshakov
66	Petr Kanko
104	Aaron Rome
115	Mark Rooneem
152	Greg Hogeboom
157	Joel Andresen
185	Ryan Murphy
215	Mikhail Lyubushin
248	Tuukka Pulliainen
279	Connor James

2001

18	Jens Karlsson
30	David Steckel
49	Michael Cammalleri
51	Jaroslav Bednar
83	Henrik Juntunen
116	Richard Petiot
152	Terry Denike
153	Tuukka Mantyla
214	Cristobal Huet
237	Mike Gabinet
277	Sebastien Laplante

2000

20	Alexander Frolov
54	Andreas Lilja
86	Yanick Lehoux
118	Lubomir Visnovsky
165	Nathan Marsters
201	Evgeny Fedorov
206	Tim Eriksson
218	Craig Olynick
245	Dan Welch
250	Flavien Conne
282	Carl Grahn

1999

43	Andrei Shefer
74	Jason Crain
76	Frantisek Kaberle
92	Cory Campbell
104	Brian McGrattan
125	Daniel Johansson
133	Jean-Francois Nogues
193	Kevin Baker
222	George Parros
250	Noah Clarke

1998

21	Mathieu Biron
46	Justin Papineau
76	Alexei Volkov
103	Kip Brennan
133	Joe Rullier
163	Tomas Zizka
190	Tommi Hannus
217	Jim Henkel
248	Matthew Yeats

1997

3	Olli Jokinen
15	Matt Zultek
29	Scott Barney
83	Joe Corvo
99	Sean Blanchard
137	Richard Seeley
150	Jeff Katcher
193	Jay Kopischke
220	Konrad Brand

1996

30	Josh Green
37	Marian Cisar
57	Greg Phillips
84	Mikael Simons
96	Eric Belanger
120	Jesse Black
123	Peter Hogan
190	Steve Valiquette
193	Kai Nurminen
219	Sebastien Simard

1995

3	Aki Berg
33	Donald MacLean
50	Pavel Rosa
59	Vladimir Tsyplakov
118	Jason Morgan
137	Igor Melyakov
157	Benoit Larose
163	Juha Vuorivirta
215	Brian Stewart

1994

7	Jamie Storr
33	Matt Johnson
59	Vitali Yachmenev
111	Chris Schmidt

163	Luc Gagne
189	Andrew Dale
215	Jan Nemecek
241	Sergei Shalamai

1993

42	Shayne Toporowski
68	Jeff Mitchell
94	Bob Wren
105	Frederik Beaubien
117	Jason Saal
146	Jere Karalahti
172	Justin Martin
198	Travis Dillabough
224	Martin Strbak
250	Kimmo Timonen
276	Patrick Howald

1992

39	Justin Hocking
63	Sandy Allan
87	Kevin Brown
111	Jeff Shevalier
135	Raymond Murray
207	Magnus Wernblom
231	Ryan Pisiak
255	Jukka Tiilikainen

1991

42	Guy Leveque
79	Keith Redmond
81	Alexei Zhitnik
108	Pauli Jaks
130	Brett Seguin
152	Kelly Fairchild
196	Craig Brown
218	Mattias Olsson
240	Andre Boulianne
262	Michael Gaul

1990

7	Darryl Sydor
28	Brandy Semchuk
49	Bob Berg
91	David Goverde
112	Erik Andersson
133	Robert Lang
154	Dean Hulett
175	Dennis LeBlanc
196	Patric Ross

217	Kevin White
238	Troy Mohns

1989

39	Brent Thompson
81	Jim Maher
102	Eric Ricard
103	Thomas Newman
123	Daniel Rydmark
144	Ted Kramer
165	Sean Whyte
182	Jim Giacin
186	Martin Maskarinec
207	Jim Hiller
228	Steve Jaques
249	Kevin Sneddon

1988

7	Martin Gelinas
28	Paul Holden
49	John Van Kessel
70	Rob Blake
91	Jeff Robison
109	Micah Aivazoff
112	Robert Larsson
133	Jeff Kruesel
154	Timo Peltomaa
175	Jim Larkin
196	Brad Hyatt
217	Doug Laprade
238	Joe Flanagan

1987

4	Wayne McBean
27	Mark Fitzpatrick
43	Ross Wilson
90	Mike Vukonich
111	Greg Batters
132	Kyosti Karjalainen
174	Jeff Gawlicki
195	John Preston
216	Rotislav Vlach
237	Mikael Lindholm

1986

2	Jimmy Carson
44	Denis Larocque
65	Sylvain Couturier
86	Ben Ferriera
107	Robb Stauber

128	Sean Krakiwsky
149	Rene Chapdelaine
170	Trevor Pochipinski
191	Paul Kelly
212	Russ Mann
233	Brian Hayton

1985

9	Craig Duncanson
10	Dan Gratton
30	Par Edlund
72	Perry Florio
93	Petr Prajsler
135	Tim Flanagan
156	John Hyduke
177	Steve Horner
219	Trent Ciprick
240	Marian Horvath

1984

6	Craig Redmond
24	Brian Wilks
48	John English
69	Tom Glavine
87	David Grannis
108	Greg Strome
129	Tim Hanley
150	Shannon Deegan
171	Luc Robitaille
191	Jeff Crossman
212	Paul Kenny
232	Brian Martin

1983

47	Bruce Shoebottom
67	Guy Benoit
87	Bob Laforest
100	Garry Galley
107	Dave Lundmark
108	Kevin Stevens
127	Tim Burgess
147	Ken Hammond
167	Bruce Fishback
187	Thomas Ahlen
207	Jan Blaha
227	Chad Johnson

1982

27	Mike Heidt
48	Steve Seguin
64	Dave Gans
82	Dave Ross
90	Darcy Roy
95	Ulf Isaksson
132	Victor Nechayev
153	Peter Helander
174	Dave Chartier
195	John Franzosa
216	Ray Shero
237	Mats Ullander

1981

2	Doug Smith
39	Dean Kennedy
81	Marty Dallman
123	Brad Thompson
134	Craig Hurley
144	Peter Sawkins
165	Dan Brennan
186	Al Tuer
207	Jeff Baikie

1980

4	Larry Murphy
10	Jim Fox
33	Greg Terrion
34	Dave Morrison
52	Steve Bozek
73	Bernie Nicholls
94	Alan Graves
115	Darren Eliot
136	Mike O'Connor
157	Billy O'Dwyer
178	Daryl Evans
199	Kim Collins

1979

16	Jay Wells
29	Dean Hopkins
30	Mark Hardy
50	John-Paul Kelly
71	John Gibson
92	Jim Brown
113	Jay McFarlane

1978

77	Paul Mancini
94	Doug Keans
111	Don Waddell
128	Bob Mierkalns
145	Rick Scully
162	Brad Thiessen
177	Jim Armstrong
193	Claude Larochelle

1977

84	Julian Baretta
85	Warren Holmes
103	Randy Rudnyk
120	Bob Suter

1976

21	Steve Clippingdale
49	Don Moores
67	Bob Mears
85	Rob Palmer
103	Larry McRae

1975

16	Tim Young
33	Terry Bucyk
69	Andre Leduc
87	Dave Miglia
105	Bob Russell
123	Dave Faulkner
141	Bill Reber
157	Sean Sullivan
172	Brian Petrovek
186	Tom Goddard
197	Mario Viens
203	Chuck Carpenter
207	Bob Fish
210	Dave Taylor
213	Bob Shaw

1974

48	Gary Sargent
66	Brad Winton
84	Paul Evans
102	Marty Mathews
120	Harvey Stewart
137	John Held
154	Mario Lessard
169	Derrick Emerson
184	Jacques Locas

197	Lindsay Thomson
207	Craig Brickley
217	Brad Kuglin

1973

38	Russ Walker
54	Jim McCrimmon
70	Dennis Abgrall
86	Blair MacDonald
102	Roly Kimble

1972

20	Don Kozak
36	Dave Hutchison
52	John Dobie
68	Bernie Germain
84	Mike Usitalo
100	Glen Toner

1971

34	Vic Venasky
48	Neil Komadoski
62	Gary Crosby
76	Camille LaPierre
89	Peter Harasym
90	Norm Dube
103	Lorne Stamler

1970

24	Al McDonough
38	Terry Holbrook
59	Billy Smith
73	Gerry Bradbury
86	Brian Carlin
98	Brian Chinnick

1969

16	Dale Hoganson
27	Gregg Boddy
39	Bruce Landon
51	Robert "Butch" Goring

1968

7	Jim McInally

1967

1	Rick Pagnutti

Bernier, Jonathan

b. Laval, Quebec, August 7, 1988

Goalie – catches left

5'11" 186 lbs.

Drafted 11th overall by Los Angeles in 2006

Jonathan Bernier was only 16 when he joined the Lewiston Maineiacs of the Quebec Major Junior Hockey League in 2004. He spent four years playing for them while developing into a top NHL prospect. When the team made an early exit from the 2006 QMJHL playoffs, he was named the starting goalie for Canada at the U18 World Championship. He finished with a sparkling 1.71 goals-against average, although the team finished a disappointing fifth.

That summer Bernier was drafted by the Kings in the first round and a year later he made his NHL debut. His first game was played against Anaheim in London, England, as part of the league's annual season kickoff in Europe. He won that game, but was sent back to junior and played most of the rest of the year with Lewiston.

Bernier has been developed slowly by the Kings because of the emergence of Jonathan Quick as the starting goaltender. In his final year of junior Bernier made Team Canada for the U20 Worlds, helping the team win gold. In 2008–09, Bernier played with the Manchester Monarchs of the AHL and, in his second season on the farm team, he was named the AHL's best goalie.

After the Kings' early playoff exit in 2011, Bernier again represented Canada, this time at the senior World Championship. He played in three games and allowed only six goals. This past season, with Quick firmly entrenched as the number-one man, Bernier managed to get into 16 games. The L.A. Kings allowed the second fewest goals in the 2011–12 season (179), making a strong argument for the Quick–Bernier combination being one of the best goaltending tandems in the NHL.

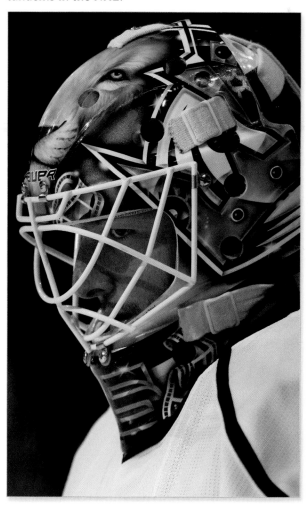

Career Statistics		Regular Season						Playoffs					
		GP	W-L-O/T	Mins	GA	SO	GAA	GP	W-L	Mins	GA	SO	GAA
2007–08	LA	4	1–3–0	238	16	0	4.03			DNQ			
2009–10	LA	3	3–0–0	185	4	1	1.30			DNP			
2010–11	LA	25	11–8–3	1,378	57	3	2.48			DNP			
2011–12	LA	16	5–6–2	890	35	1	2.36		for 2012 playoff stats see p. 18				
NHL Totals		48	20–17–5	2,692	112	5	2.50	—	—	—	—	—	—

Brown, Dustin

b. Ithaca, New York, November 4, 1984

Left wing – shoots right

6'0" 208 lbs.

Drafted 13th overall by Los Angeles in 2003

Kings' captain Dustin Brown has played his entire, nine-season NHL career in Los Angeles. A leader by example, he developed with the Guelph Storm of the Ontario Hockey League into a strong, two-way player.

Brown's quest to become an NHL regular was delayed by two events. First, during his rookie season of 2003–04, he suffered an ankle injury after only 31 games and missed the rest of the season. And second, the NHL lockout in 2004–05 put off his return another year. Perhaps this time was a blessing in disguise, as Brown spent the year with the Kings' AHL affiliate in Manchester, where he averaged a point a game and continued to develop his play.

During his junior days, Brown represented the U.S. in consecutive U20 tournaments, 2002 and 2003, and he was a key player in the nation's bronze medal win at the 2004 senior World Championship. His breakout year in the NHL came in 2007–08 when he had 33 goals playing on a line with scoring sensation Anze Kopitar. He has had at least 22 goals each season since.

Prior to 2012, the Kings struggled to find playoff success. When his team failed to qualify for the postseason, Brown was a proud participant for USA Hockey at the World Championship. After the 2004 medal, he played again in 2006, 2008, and 2009.

Because of his dedication to the national team and his success in Los Angeles, he was named to the U.S. Olympic team for Vancouver 2010. He helped his country win a silver medal and, on returning to the NHL, led the Kings to their first playoff berth in seven years.

Brown was named the Kings' captain in 2008 at age 23, the youngest man to wear the "C" in franchise history and also the first American to be granted the honour.

Career Statistics		Regular Season					Playoffs				
		GP	G	A	P	Pim	GP	G	A	P	Pim
2003–04	LA	31	1	4	5	16			DNQ		
2004–05	LA			No Season							
2005–06	LA	79	14	14	28	80			DNQ		
2006–07	LA	81	17	29	46	54			DNQ		
2007–08	LA	78	33	27	60	55			DNQ		
2008–09	LA	80	24	29	53	64			DNQ		
2009–10	LA	82	24	32	56	41	6	1	4	5	6
2010–11	LA	82	28	29	57	67	6	1	1	2	6
2011–12	LA	82	22	32	54	53			for 2012 playoff stats see p. 18		
NHL Totals		595	163	196	359	430	12	2	5	7	12

Carter, Jeff

b. London, Ontario, January 1, 1985

Centre – shoots right

6'4" 200 lbs.

Drafted 11th overall by Philadelphia in 2003

Jeff Carter was a highly-touted junior prospect who ended up being drafted in the first round by the Flyers in 2003. He had a stellar career with Sault Ste. Marie in the Ontario Hockey League from 2001 to 2005, scoring over 30 goals in each season after his rookie year. When his career with the Greyhounds ended, he went directly to the Philadelphia Phantoms, the Flyers' AHL affiliate, where he helped the team win the Calder Cup in 2005. Carter was no standby player in those playoffs, scoring 23 points in 21 games.

Carter made the Flyers at training camp in 2005. He netted 23 goals as a rookie, garnering several votes for the Calder Trophy in a year dominated by two other superstar rookies: Sidney Crosby and Alex Ovechkin.

It was Carter's fourth season that elevated him to elite status throughout the league, as Philadelphia's patience in developing him was rewarded with a breakout season. Carter had 46 goals and 84 points in the regular season, though the team lost in the opening round of the playoffs.

In the summer of 2011, the Columbus Blue Jackets made an impression by acquiring Carter from the Flyers. He would struggle with injuries during his time with the Jackets, just as the team struggled to win games. After 39 games in Ohio, Carter was traded to Los Angeles for top defenceman Jack Johnson and a 2012 first-round draft choice. The move to California helped Carter find his game again, and he became a key player in the King's postseason.

In addition to his NHL career, Carter has won gold with Canada's U18 and U20 teams and played at the 2006 World Championship.

Career Statistics		Regular Season					Playoffs				
		GP	G	A	P	Pim	GP	G	A	P	Pim
2005–06	PHI	81	23	19	42	40	6	0	0	0	0
2006–07	PHI	62	14	23	37	48			DNQ		
2007–08	PHI	82	29	24	53	55	17	6	5	11	12
2008–09	PHI	82	46	38	84	68	6	1	0	1	8
2009–10	PHI	74	33	28	61	38	12	5	2	7	2
2010–11	PHI	80	36	30	66	39	6	1	1	2	2
2011–12	CBJ/LA	55	21	13	34	16		for 2012 playoff stats see p. 18			
NHL Totals		516	202	175	377	304	47	13	8	21	24

Clifford, Kyle

b. Ayr, Ontario, January 13, 1991

Left wing – shoots left

6'2" 200 lbs.

Drafted 35th overall by Los Angeles in 2009

A gritty and tough left winger who graduated from the Barrie Colts of the Ontario Hockey League, Kyle Clifford was the Kings' second-round draft choice three years ago. In the 2009–10 season, his final year of junior, Clifford represented Canada at the U18 World Championship, placing fourth. He finished that season playing for Manchester in the AHL playoffs.

Clifford made the Kings out of training camp in 2010 while still only 19 years old. Considered a third- or fourth-line player, he has some offensive talent while playing the role of dogged checker. He didn't see much action in the 2012 playoffs, as coach Sutter chose to go with experience during the critical run to the Cup.

Career Statistics		Regular Season					Playoffs				
		GP	G	A	P	Pim	GP	G	A	P	Pim
2010–11	LA	76	7	7	14	141	6	3	2	5	0
2011–12	LA	81	5	7	12	123	for 2012 playoff stats see p. 18				
NHL Totals		157	12	14	26	264	6	3	2	5	0

Doughty, Drew

b. London, Ontario, December 8, 1989

Defence – shoots right

6'0'' 211 lbs.

Drafted 2nd overall by Los Angeles in 2008

Drew Doughty is arguably the best young defenceman in the NHL – or one of its best defencemen, period. Still only 22, he has been in the league four years, won medals at three levels of international play, and is the core of a Los Angeles team that looks to continue to dominate for many years to come.

Doughty is a blend of modern player and Bobby Orr–style defenceman. A brilliant skater with tons of offensive ability from the blue line, he can single-handedly control a game by changing the tempo of his skating. He is a sure puck handler and plays a more mature game than his age suggests.

After only three years in the Ontario Hockey League it was clear Doughty could play in the NHL. He joined the Kings straight out of junior in 2008, and, as an 18-year-old, stepped into the lineup as though he had always been there. His brilliant rookie season garnered many votes for the Calder Trophy, and he followed with a sophomore season that suggested superstardom was at hand. In his second year, Doughty doubled his point production, reversed his plus/minus from minus-17 to plus-20, and became the lynchpin of a young team with nothing but promise.

After a drop in production in his third and fourth seasons, Doughty silenced any critics with a sensational playoff performance in 2012. In addition to his remarkable success in the NHL, he also led Canada to gold at the U20 in 2008. A year later he played at the senior World Championships, where Canada lost to Russia in the gold-medal game and had to settle for silver. In 2010 he played for his country again, this time at the Olympics.

Career Statistics		Regular Season					Playoffs				
		GP	G	A	P	Pim	GP	G	A	P	Pim
2008–09	LA	81	6	21	27	56					
2009–10	LA	82	16	43	59	54	6	3	4	7	4
2010–11	LA	76	11	29	40	68	6	2	2	4	8
2011–12	LA	77	10	26	36	69	for 2012 playoff stats see p. 18				
NHL Totals		316	43	119	162	247	12	5	6	11	12

Fraser, Colin

b. Surrey, British Columbia, January 28, 1985

Centre – shoots left

6'1" 190 lbs.

Drafted 69th overall by Philadelphia in 2003

Colin Fraser was traded by his draft team before ever playing in the NHL. Now in the prime of his career, Fraser brings with him to Los Angeles a measure of both success and experience that are essential to the chemistry of any winning team.

A Western Hockey League boy, Fraser played junior with the Red Deer Rebels and was drafted by Philadelphia in 2003. The lockout prevented him from making a run at the Flyers' main roster, but he developed in junior and then the American Hockey League, eventually being acquired by Chicago. The Hawks kept him in the minors, and it was there the persistent Fraser spent the next four years trying to realize his NHL dream.

Although he played one game in 2006–07, Fraser didn't make the Blackhawks on a permanent basis until the 2008–09 season. The reliable centreman was on the team for two years, including 2009–10 when the Blackhawks won their first Stanley Cup since 1961. That summer, though, he was traded to Edmonton. After a year in Alberta, he was acquired by the Kings in a deal that brought Ryan Smyth back to the Oilers.

Fraser also played on the Sidney Crosby–led U20 Canadian team that won a gold medal in 2005 by crushing Russia 6–1 in the final game.

Career Statistics	Regular Season					Playoffs				
	GP	G	A	P	Pim	GP	G	A	P	Pim
2006–07 CHI	1	0	0	0	2	DNP				
2007–08 CHI	5	0	0	0	7	DNP				
2008–09 CHI	81	6	11	17	55	2	0	0	0	2
2009–10 CHI	70	7	12	19	44	3	0	0	0	0
2010–11 EDM	67	3	2	5	60	DNQ				
2011–12 LA	67	2	6	8	67	for 2012 playoff stats see p. 18				
NHL Totals	291	18	31	49	235	5	0	0	0	2

Gagne, Simon

b. Ste. Foy, Quebec, February 29, 1980

Left wing – shoots left

6'1" 195 lbs.

Drafted 22nd overall by Philadelphia in 1998

At 32, Simon Gagne is one of the veterans on the Kings. He has had a sensational career both in the NHL and the international arena. He played three years in the Quebec Major Junior Hockey League, earning himself a first-round draft selection in 1998, which he followed with a memorable final year in junior as he led the league in goals (50) and points (120). He also scored four goals in one game for Canada at the U20 in Winnipeg, helping the team to a silver medal.

Gagne made the Flyers in 1999 and has been a mainstay in the NHL ever since. He scored 20 goals as a rookie and increased those numbers to 27 and 33 in the next two seasons playing on a line with Keith Primeau and Mark Recchi. He quickly established himself as one of the most consistent scorers in the game. After the lockout he had a career high goal-scoring season, netting 47, followed by 41 the next year. As a result, he earned a five-year, $25-million contract with the team. His career suffered a setback in 2007–08 when the lingering effects of several concussions caused him to play only 25 games.

He returned with some success, but injuries limited his effectiveness and he was traded to Tampa Bay. In the summer of 2011 he became a free agent and decided to sign with the Kings. Another concussion ended his season after 34 games and he missed the playoffs entirely.

Gagne also played for Canada on the championship team at the 2004 World Cup of Hockey. Two years earlier, he won gold with the country's Olympic team in Salt Lake. He also won a silver medal at the 2005 World Championship.

Career Statistics		Regular Season					Playoffs				
		GP	G	A	P	Pim	GP	G	A	P	Pim
1999–2000	PHI	80	20	28	48	22	17	5	5	10	2
2000–01	PHI	69	27	32	59	18	6	3	0	3	0
2001–02	PHI	79	33	33	66	32	5	0	0	0	2
2002–03	PHI	46	9	18	27	16	13	4	1	5	6
2003–04	PHI	80	24	21	45	29	18	5	4	9	12
2004–05	PHI		No Season								
2005–06	PHI	72	47	32	79	38	6	3	1	4	2
2006–07	PHI	76	41	27	68	30		DNQ			
2007–08	PHI	25	7	11	18	4		DNP			
2008–09	PHI	79	34	40	74	42	6	3	1	4	2
2009–10	PHI	58	17	23	40	47	19	9	3	12	0
2010–11	TB	63	17	23	40	20	15	5	7	12	4
2011–12	LA	34	7	10	17	18	for 2012 playoff stats see p. 18				
NHL Totals		761	283	298	581	316	105	37	22	59	30

Greene, Matt

b. Grand Ledge, Michigan, May 13, 1983

Defence – shoots right

6'3" 237 lbs.

Drafted 44th overall by Edmonton in 2002

Few players are as multi-faceted as Matt Greene. A collegian with plenty of international experience as a member of Team USA, he is also a large and intimidating force on the blue line. He played at the University of North Dakota for three years (2002–05) and led the Western Collegiate Hockey Association in penalty minutes twice. His advanced abilities drew the attention of the Oilers, who enticed him to leave the college ranks a year early and turn pro.

In 2005–06, Greene split his first season with the Oilers and their farm team in Iowa. At the end of his rookie season he was called up by Edmonton permanently as the team made a run to the Stanley Cup Final, losing in Game 7 to the Carolina Hurricanes.

Greene established himself as a physical force for the Oilers, one who could dictate play in his own end by using his size and strength. Never a prolific scorer – he has just 11 goals in more than 450 career games – it's his defensive abilities that have garnered rave reviews. In 2008, Greene was traded to the Kings, along with Jarrett Stoll, in exchange for Lubomir Visnovsky.

In addition to his NHL career, Greene played at both the U18 and U20 tournaments for USA Hockey and has played in three World Championships – 2007, 2008, and 2010. He recently signed a five-year contract extension with the Kings, ensuring the team's defensive end will continue to be a pillar of strength for years to come.

Career Statistics		Regular Season					Playoffs				
		GP	G	A	P	Pim	GP	G	A	P	Pim
2005–06	EDM	27	0	2	2	43	18	0	1	1	34
2006–07	EDM	78	1	9	10	109			DNQ		
2007–08	EDM	46	0	1	1	53			DNQ		
2008–09	LA	82	2	12	14	111			DNQ		
2009–10	LA	75	2	7	9	83	6	0	1	1	0
2010–11	LA	71	2	9	11	70	6	0	0	0	14
2011–12	LA	82	4	11	15	58	for 2012 playoff stats see p. 18				
NHL Totals		461	11	51	62	527	30	0	2	2	48

Hunter, Trent

b. Red Deer, Alberta, July 5, 1980

Right wing – shoots right

6'3" 210 lbs.

Drafted 150th overall by Anaheim in 1998

An unlikely success story, Trent Hunter came to the Kings after a decade in pro hockey. He made his NHL debut with the Islanders during the 2002 playoffs after a successful junior career with Prince George of the Western Hockey League.

Hunter spent most of his first two years of pro hockey in the AHL. In 2003–04 he had a breakout season with the Islanders, scoring 25 goals and 51 points, both tied for tops on the team. He played in Sweden during the lockout and returned a year later as good as ever. Never the superstar on the team, he was nonetheless capable of scoring and playing a hard-nosed game, giving his coach valuable minutes on ice without being a liability.

After nearly a decade with the team Hunter was traded to New Jersey in the summer of 2011. The Devils then put him on waivers, and he signed with the Kings before ever playing a game in Jersey. Picking up Hunter proved to be another shrewd move by L.A. management in their quest to assemble a Stanley Cup–contending team.

Career Statistics		Regular Season					Playoffs				
		GP	G	A	P	Pim	GP	G	A	P	Pim
2001–02	NYI		DNP				4	1	1	2	2
2002–03	NYI	8	0	0	0	4		DNP			
2003–04	NYI	77	25	26	51	16	5	0	0	0	4
2004–05	NYI		No Season								
2005–06	NYI	82	16	19	35	34		DNQ			
2006–07	NYI	77	20	15	35	22	5	3	0	3	0
2007–08	NYI	82	12	29	41	43		DNQ			
2008–09	NYI	55	14	17	31	41		DNQ			
2009–10	NYI	61	11	17	28	18		DNQ			
2010–11	NYI	17	1	3	4	23		DNQ			
2011–12	LA	38	2	5	7	8	for 2012 playoff stats see p. 18				
NHL Totals		497	101	135	236	209	14	4	1	5	6

King, Dwight

b. Meadow Lake, Saskatchewan, July 5, 1989

Left wing – shoots left

6'3" 234 lbs.

Drafted 109th overall by Los Angeles in 2007

Dwight King is the younger brother of D.J. King, who currently plays with the Washington Capitals. Dwight started junior hockey at the age of 15 and played five years with the Lethbridge Hurricanes of the Western Hockey League. It was during this time that the Kings used a mid-range draft choice to get him into their system.

King worked his way up through the ranks. He started 2009–10 in the East Coast Hockey League, was promoted to the American Hockey League early in the season, and after another year with Manchester got into his first NHL game.

That moment occurred on November 17, 2010, when King was an emergency replacement for an injured Alexei Ponikarovsky. He played six games that season and another 27 this past year. He proved himself so invaluable during his time with the Kings this season that his presence in the 2012 Cup playoffs was a given every night.

King has had to earn every shift he gets in the NHL, and he has proved more than capable. He is a disciplined player who can adapt to any role the coach chooses to assign him. .

Career Statistics		Regular Season					Playoffs				
		GP	G	A	P	Pim	GP	G	A	P	Pim
2010–11	LA	6	0	0	0	2	DNQ				
2011–12	LA	27	5	9	14	10	for 2012 playoff stats see p. 18				
NHL Totals		33	5	9	14	12	—	—	—	—	—

Kopitar, Anze

b. Jesenice, Yugoslavia (Slovenia),
 August 24, 1987

Centre – shoots left

6'3" 222 lbs.

Drafted 11th overall by Los Angeles in 2005

Anze Kopitar holds a truly unique place in hockey history. He comes from a small country that has absolutely no history of producing world-class hockey players. Despite this, he knew early on he wanted to play the game, and he knew he'd have to leave home to do it. There were simply no players or coaches of world-class calibre in his homeland of Slovenia.

Kopitar's first taste of hockey came from his father, who played pro in Slovenia and who built a rink in the family's backyard during winter. Kopitar loved skating, and his father helped nurture that love. As the child got bigger and more skilled, it was clear he was outgrowing the country's hockey program.

Kopitar's first step toward the NHL was a move to Sweden to play with Södertälje of the Swedish Elite League. There he played alongside like-skilled players and was spotted by many NHL scouts. The Kings drafted him a lofty 11th overall and, after one more year in Sweden, he attended the Kings' training camp in 2006, just after his 19th birthday.

It was clear from day one he had found his home. Kopitar had the skill and strength, the determination, size, and shot to be a top-line forward with Los Angeles. He had 20 goals and 61 points as a rookie and since that year has never failed to score fewer than 25 goals. In 2011–12, he scored 76 points, the fourth straight year he finished tops in points for the team.

At the start of the 2008–09 season he signed a seven-year, $47-million contract extension, and he has given the team everything it expected of him. Consistent and tenacious, he is a fighter and survivor, a gritty player who can come out of the corner with the puck and snap a shot from the slot with equal effectiveness. The Kings' lengthy playoff run in 2012 is unquestionably connected to his rise as one of the top players in the game.

Career Statistics		Regular Season					Playoffs				
		GP	G	A	P	Pim	GP	G	A	P	Pim
2006–07	LA	72	20	41	61	24	DNQ				
2007–08	LA	82	32	45	77	22	DNQ				
2008–09	LA	82	27	39	66	32	DNQ				
2009–10	LA	82	34	47	81	16	6	2	3	5	2
2010–11	LA	75	25	48	73	20	DNQ				
2011–12	LA	82	25	51	76	20	for 2012 playoff stats see p. 18				
NHL Totals		475	163	271	434	134	6	2	3	5	2

Lewis, Trevor

b. Salt Lake City, Utah, January 8, 1987

Centre – shoots right

6'0'' 200 lbs.

Drafted 17th overall by Los Angeles in 2006

Lewis was drafted in the first round by the Kings in 2006, having just completed his second year with Des Moines in the United States Hockey League. From there he transferred to Owen Sound of the Ontario Hockey League. The Kings, however, saw big things for Lewis and moved him to Manchester of the AHL after less than a season.

Lewis spent the next three years with the Monarchs (2007–10) and finally made the Kings in the fall of 2010. He has been mostly a fourth-liner, but has embraced his role and been effective in that capacity. He has proved to be exactly the kind of player coach Darryl Sutter considers critical to winning the Cup and was in the lineup throughout the 2012 playoff run.

Career Statistics		Regular Season					Playoffs				
		GP	G	A	P	Pim	GP	G	A	P	Pim
2008–09	LA	6	1	2	3	0			DNQ		
2009–10	LA	5	0	0	0	0			DNP		
2010–11	LA	72	3	10	13	6	6	1	3	4	2
2011–12	LA	72	3	4	7	26		for 2012 playoff stats see p. 18			
NHL Totals		155	7	16	23	32	6	1	3	4	2

Loktionov, Andrei

b. Voskresensk, Russia, May 30, 1990

Centre – shoots left

5'10" 180 lbs.

Drafted 123rd overall by Los Angeles in 2008

One of two Russians on the Kings (with Slava Voynov), Andrei Loktionov is a young player who has had a slow start to his NHL career. He was a mid-round draft choice by L.A., chosen based on his play in Russia and at the U18 tournament, who is trying to develop into a scoring centreman.

Loktionov starred with Russia at the U18 in 2007 and 2008, winning a gold and silver medal and scoring five goals. In the fall of 2008 he left Yaroslavl of the Kontinental Hockey League to play for Windsor in the Ontario Hockey League. He showed tremendous signs of progress, averaging more than a point a game, and helped the Spitfires to a Memorial Cup win. In 2009, he made the Kings at training camp.

His career hit a snag on November 26, 2009, when he suffered a shoulder injury that required surgery and put him off the ice for several months. When he was healthy, the Kings sent him to Manchester, and it is there he has spent most of his career to date.

Career Statistics		Regular Season					Playoffs				
		GP	G	A	P	Pim	GP	G	A	P	Pim
2009–10	LA	1	0	0	0	0	DNP				
2010–11	LA	19	4	3	7	2	DNP				
2011–12	LA	39	3	4	7	2	for 2012 playoff stats see p. 18				
NHL Totals		59	7	7	14	4	—	—	—	—	—

Martinez, Alec

b. Rochester Hills, Michigan, July 26, 1987

Defence – shoots left

6'1" 208 lbs.

Drafted 95th overall by Los Angeles in 2007

Alec Martinez cut his teeth in the Central Collegiate Hockey Association with the Miami University Redhawks between 2004 and 2008. It was during this time that the strong-skating defenceman attracted the attention of the Kings, who drafted him in the fourth round in 2007.

After starting 2009–10 with the Kings, Martinez was sent down to Manchester for the balance of the season to develop. For the last two seasons he has spent more time in the NHL than the AHL, a sure sign of progress. He has shown a good combination of size and skill on the blue line and is certainly a feel-good story who has made a solid and impressive contribution to the team's Stanley Cup run in 2012.

Career Statistics		Regular Season					Playoffs				
		GP	G	A	P	Pim	GP	G	A	P	Pim
2009–10	LA	4	0	0	0	2	DNP				
2010–11	LA	60	5	11	16	18	6	0	1	1	2
2011–12	LA	51	6	6	12	8	for 2012 playoff stats see p. 18				
NHL Totals		115	11	17	28	28	6	0	1	1	2

Mitchell, Willie

b. Port McNeill, British Columbia, April 23, 1977

Defence – shoots left

6'3" 208 lbs.

Drafted 199th overall by New Jersey in 1996

At 35, and as one of the elder statesman on the Kings, Willie Mitchell has been there and back and knows how far it is. Indeed, his life in hockey has been about adapting and re-adapting. Even as a kid, he started on ice as a figure skater before switching to hockey, and when he played hockey, he started as a forward before moving back to defence.

In the mid-1990s, Mitchell played provincial junior hockey before getting a scholarship offer to play for the Clarkson Knights of the Eastern Collegiate Athletic Conference. This was 1997, a year after he had been a low draft choice by the Devils. It wasn't much encouragement, but it was enough to give Mitchell the needed inner desire to reach for the stars.

He spent the first three years of his pro career (1998–2001) mostly in the minors, but he did get into 18 games for New Jersey to get his NHL career on track. After his time with the Devils, he was traded to Minnesota in a move that did him a world of good. The Wild needed a defensive defenceman, and he fit the bill perfectly. He averaged more than 20 minutes of playing time a game and was almost always a plus player.

Mitchell signed with Vancouver in 2006 and became one of the team's leaders. After four years with the Canucks he moved down the coast to play with Los Angeles. Often paired with Drew Doughty, the duo form the backbone of the team's defence, despite Mitchell having missed 25 games over the season due to a series of hard-luck injuries. In the playoffs he was a rock in his own end.

Internationally, he helped Canada win gold at the 2004 World Championship.

Career Statistics		Regular Season					Playoffs				
		GP	G	A	P	Pim	GP	G	A	P	Pim
1999–2000	NJ	2	0	0	0	0			DNP		
2000–01	NJ/MIN	33	1	9	10	40			DNQ		
2001–02	MIN	68	3	10	13	68			DNQ		
2002–03	MIN	69	2	12	14	84	18	1	3	4	14
2003–04	MIN	70	1	13	14	83			DNQ		
2004–05	MIN			No Season							
2005–06	MIN/DAL	80	2	8	10	113	5	0	0	0	2
2006–07	VAN	62	1	10	11	45	12	0	1	1	12
2007–08	VAN	72	2	10	12	81			DNP		
2008–09	VAN	82	3	20	23	59	10	0	2	2	22
2009–10	VAN	48	4	8	12	48			DNP		
2010–11	LA	57	5	5	10	21	6	1	1	2	4
2011–12	LA	76	5	19	24	44		for 2012 playoff stats see p. 18				
NHL Totals		719	29	124	153	686	51	2	7	9	54

Moreau, Ethan

b. Huntsville, Ontario, September 22, 1975

Left wing – shoots left

6'2" 220 lbs.

Drafted 14th overall by Chicago in 1994

The oldest player on the Kings, Ethan Moreau's leadership abilities are a key component of a young team like the Kings.

It was during an outstanding junior career with Niagara Falls of the Ontario Hockey League that Chicago spotted Moreau and decided to draft him in the first round in 1994. He made the leap to the International Hockey League a year later and, by training camp in 1996, he established himself as a young star in the game.

Moreau had size, speed, and skill, and although his scoring touch wasn't his greatest asset, he was a complete hockey player. He played four years with the Hawks before being traded to Edmonton, and it was there he spent the prime of his career, some eleven years in all.

At the start of the 2007–08 season he was named Oilers' captain, but one day later he broke his leg. This started a difficult time during which he played just 32 games over two years. He rebounded to resume a prominent role with the Oilers, but in 2010 he was put on waivers and claimed by Columbus. After one injury-shortened year with the Blue Jackets, the Kings signed him as a free agent. Although he was limited to just 28 games this past regular season, the respect he brings to the dressing room can't help but rub off on his teammates and contribute to the team's winning ways.

Career Statistics		Regular Season					Playoffs				
		GP	G	A	P	Pim	GP	G	A	P	Pim
1995–96	CHI	8	0	1	1	4			DNP		
1996–97	CHI	82	15	16	31	123	6	1	0	1	9
1997–98	CHI	54	9	9	18	73			DNQ		
1998–99	CHI/EDM	80	10	11	21	92	4	0	3	3	6
1999–2000	EDM	73	17	10	27	62	5	0	1	1	0
2000–01	EDM	68	9	10	19	90	4	0	0	0	2
2001–02	EDM	80	11	5	16	81			DNQ		
2002–03	EDM	78	14	17	31	112	6	0	1	1	16
2003–04	EDM	81	20	12	32	96			DNQ		
2004–05	EDM			No Season							
2005–06	EDM	74	11	16	27	87	21	2	1	3	19
2006–07	EDM	7	1	0	1	12			DNQ		
2007–08	EDM	25	5	4	9	39			DNQ		
2008–09	EDM	77	14	12	26	133			DNQ		
2009–10	EDM	76	9	9	18	62			DNQ		
2010–11	CBJ	37	1	5	6	24			DNQ		
2011–12	LA	28	1	3	4	20		for 2012 playoff stats see p. 18			
NHL Totals		928	147	140	287	1,110	46	3	6	9	52

Nolan, Jordan

b. St. Catharines, Ontario, June 23, 1989

Centre – shoots left

6'3" 216 lbs.

Drafted 186th overall by Los Angeles in 2009

There's still a long way to go before we know what Jordan Nolan's NHL career will be like, but with his pedigree he has a good chance to be successful. The son of former player and coach Ted Nolan, Jordan was a late draft choice by the Kings in 2009. Rather than take his late selection as a negative, he used it as motivation to make the NHL.

Nolan played for three teams in the Ontario Hockey League during his junior career (2005–10), after which the Kings assigned him to Manchester to develop. On February 11, 2012, he was called up by the Kings to play in his first NHL game. Just 24 hours later he scored the first goal of his career. He remained with the club for the remainder of the regular season and throughout the playoffs, scoring a goal against St. Louis in the Kings' four-game sweep of the Blues.

Still young and unproven, Nolan has nonetheless risen to each challenge he has faced and shows promise that his might prove to be a lengthy NHL career.

Career Statistics		Regular Season					Playoffs				
		GP	G	A	P	Pim	GP	G	A	P	Pim
2011–12	LA	26	2	2	4	28	for 2012 playoff stats see p. 18				
NHL Totals		26	2	2	4	28	—	—	—	—	—

Penner, Dustin

b. Winkler, Manitoba, September 28, 1982

Left wing – shoots left

6'4" 245 lbs.

Undrafted

There are few more inspirational stories than those of players who go undrafted and wind up finding success in the NHL. Dustin Penner was not only never given his due by 30 NHL teams on draft day, he also had a long history of being rejected in his early career. He was cut by several teams during his high school days, and he received so few offers of substance that his first serious hockey took place at Minot State University–Bottineau. He broke his leg before he got into a game, spent the rest of the year rehabbing, and didn't get to play until the following year.

But Penner proved too good to stay there. He was offered a scholarship to the more respected University of Maine, but had to miss a year as he transferred schools. After one impressive college season in 2003–04, the Ducks signed him as a free agent. At age 22 he was assigned to the team's AHL affiliate in Cincinnati to start his pro career.

Again, Penner rose to the occasion. In 2005–06 he played his first 19 NHL games, and the year after, all his dreams came true. Penner played the full season with Anaheim, scored 29 goals, and helped the Ducks win the Stanley Cup. Unwanted five years earlier, he was now considered one of the most promising power forwards in the league.

The result of his great year was an offer sheet from Edmonton, which the Ducks refused to match. Penner was on his way to Alberta with a five-year, $21-million contract. In three-and-a-half years with Edmonton he had a fine career, but he didn't live up to the hype of the big-time contract. The struggling Oilers traded him to Los Angeles, and he found his niche on a team that gave him a specific role that would allow him to achieve its expectations.

Penner's finest moment in the 2012 post season was scoring the overtime winner in Game 5 against Phoenix and advancing the Kings to the Stanley Cup Final for the first time since 1993.

Career Statistics		Regular Season					Playoffs				
		GP	G	A	P	Pim	GP	G	A	P	Pim
22005–06	ANA	19	4	3	7	14	13	3	6	9	12
2006–07	ANA	82	29	16	45	58	21	3	5	8	2
2007–08	EDM	82	23	24	47	45		DNQ			
2008–09	EDM	78	17	20	37	61		DNQ			
2009–10	EDM	82	32	31	63	38		DNQ			
2010–11	EDM/LA	81	23	22	45	47	6	1	1	2	4
2011–12	LA	65	7	10	17	43	for 2012 playoff stats see p. 18				
NHL Totals		489	135	126	261	306	40	7	12	19	18

Quick, Jonathan

b. Milford, Connecticut, January 21, 1986

Goalie – catches left

6'1" 223 lbs.

Drafted 72nd overall by Los Angeles in 2005

It isn't so much that Jonathan Quick's ascent has been surprising – it hasn't been – so much as it is that he has risen to the heights that he has. A solid prospect, he was drafted right out of high school after playing three years for Avon Old Farms, a prep school in New England.

Once drafted in 2005, Quick played for the University of Massachusetts for two years. Again, he improved and was a star in Hockey East, and in 2007 the Kings sent him to the minors to begin a pro career that also saw him play his first three games with the big team. Quick played partly for Reading in the East Coast Hockey League and also for Manchester in the AHL. A year later, with the Kings looking for a number-one goalie, he appeared in 44 games and posted a fine 2.48 goals-against average.

From 2009 and on, Quick has been the go-to goalie for the Kings. He has raised his profile throughout the league to the point that in 2012 he was nominated for the Vezina Trophy. He led the league with 10 shutouts in 2011–12 (also a franchise record), had a tremendous 35–21–13 record, and posted a 1.95 GAA.

Career Statistics			Regular Season						Playoffs				
		GP	W–L–O/T	Mins	GA	SO	GAA	GP	W–L	Mins	GA	SO	GAA
2007–08	LA	3	1–2–0	141	9	0	3.83			DNQ			
2008–09	LA	44	21–18–2	2,495	103	4	2.48			DNQ			
2009–10	LA	72	39–24–7	4,258	180	4	2.54	6	2–4	360	21	0	3.50
2010–11	LA	61	35–22–3	3,591	134	6	2.24	6	2–4	380	20	1	3.16
2011–12	LA	69	35–21–13	4,099	133	10	1.95			for 2012 playoff stats see p. 18			
NHL Totals		249	131–87–25	14,584	559	24	2.3	12	4–8	740	41	1	3.32

Richards, Mike

b. Kenora, Ontario, February 11, 1985

Centre – shoots left

5'11" 195 lbs.

Drafted 24th overall by Philadelphia in 2003

The assiduous acquisitions the Kings have made in the last year to solidify their team and augment their own – in many cases, young – draft choices is personified by Mike Richards. An incredible talent, he was a first-round draft choice by the Flyers in 2003 and has been a winner at every level.

As a teen, Richards played four years of junior hockey with the Kitchener Rangers, leading them to a Memorial Cup win in 2001–02. In the spring of 2005, after his final year of junior, the Flyers assigned him to their AHL affiliate, and there he helped the Phantoms win the Calder Cup championship. Richards had also won a gold and silver medal with Canada at the U20 tournament during his teenage years.

By 2005 it was clear that the 20-year-old Richards was ready for the rigours of the NHL. He increased his goal production each of his first five seasons in the big league, but he was also a sensational penalty killer and two-way player, a modern-day Bob Gainey.

After being named the Flyers' captain during training camp in 2008, Richards took the team under his wing and had his best season, scoring 80 points. A year later, the Flyers went to the Stanley Cup Final before losing in six games to Chicago. Earlier in that 2009–10 season, he was part of the Canadian national team that won Olympic gold in Vancouver.

In addition to his leadership, Richards holds a unique place in hockey history. He is the only player ever to score three goals during five-on-three situations (i.e., his team two-men short), testament to his quick hands, skating ability, and touch around the net.

The Flyers had a disappointing end to their 2010–11 season, and when the Kings realized Philadelphia GM Paul Holmgren was prepared to make some trades, they pounced, acquiring Richards in a multi-player deal that saw top prospect Brayden Schenn go the other way. The deal was costly for Los Angeles, but it gave the team an experienced player, a player whose middle name is success, and a leader who can inspire his teammates to greater heights.

Career Statistics		Regular Season					Playoffs				
		GP	G	A	P	Pim	GP	G	A	P	Pim
2005–06	PHI	79	11	23	34	65	6	0	1	1	0
2006–07	PHI	59	10	22	32	52			DNQ		
2007–08	PHI	73	28	47	75	76	17	7	7	14	10
2008–09	PHI	79	30	50	80	63	6	1	4	5	6
2009–10	PHI	82	31	31	62	79	23	7	16	23	18
2010–11	PHI	81	23	43	66	62	11	1	6	7	15
2011–12	LA	74	18	26	44	71	for 2012 playoff stats see p. 18				
NHL Totals		527	151	242	393	468	77	20	41	61	64

Richardson, Brad

b. Belleville, Ontario, February 4, 1985

Centre – shoots left

5'11" 195 lbs.

Drafted 163rd overall by Colorado in 2003

Making the most of his skills and his chances, Brad Richardson has become a perfect role player for the Kings. He is a solid third-line player who has plenty of skill and inner fire.

Richardson was a late draft choice by the Colorado Avalanche during his junior career with Owen Sound in the Ontario Hockey League. He had difficulty establishing himself with the Avs during the first three seasons of his pro career.

In the summer of 2008, he was traded to the Kings for a second-round draft choice. The move seemed to trigger new-found success for him. Injuries reduced his role in 2008–09, but since then he has been a consistent presence in the lineup for Los Angeles. He continued to do all the little things well, which is why coach Darryl Sutter continued to use him throughout the 2012 playoffs. He didn't score much, but he was a good shut-down centreman and a fearless player.

Career Statistics		Regular Season					Playoffs				
		GP	G	A	P	Pim	GP	G	A	P	Pim
2005–06	COL	41	3	10	13	12	9	1	0	1	6
2006–07	COL	73	14	8	22	28			DNQ		
2007–08	COL	22	2	3	5	8			DNP		
2008–09	LA	31	0	5	5	11			DNQ		
2009–10	LA	81	11	16	27	37	6	1	1	2	2
2010–11	LA	68	7	12	19	47	6	2	3	5	2
2011–12	LA	59	5	3	8	30		for 2012 playoff stats see p. 18			
NHL Totals		375	42	57	99	173	21	4	4	8	10

for 2012 playoff stats see p. 18

Scuderi, Rob

b. Syosset, New York, December 30, 1978

Defence – shoots left

6'1" 211 lbs.

Drafted 198th overall by Pittsburgh in 1998

Kings GM Dean Lombardi has proved incredibly savvy when it comes to signing free agents. Yet another case in point is Rob Scuderi, a name that doesn't generate buzz and excitement during the free-agent frenzy on July 1, but the kind of player a team can't win the Stanley Cup without. It was no coincidence that the Pens went to the Stanley Cup Final in 2008 and won it all in 2009 with Scuderi in the lineup.

Not flashy, not exciting, not a superstar, Scuderi is the very epitome of defensive defenceman. And Lombardi knew that, by virtue of the player's five years in Pittsburgh, he was getting a seasoned pro who practised every day with Sidney Crosby and Evgeni Malkin.

After that Cup win in 2009, Scuderi became a free agent and Lombardi snapped him up with an offer of four years and $13.6 million. Given that he had six goals in 537 regular-season games, it is clear Scuderi wasn't being counted on for offence from the blue line. Both men well understood, however, what an important signing this was. And Scuderi hasn't disappointed. He continues to play the man, block shots, and lead by example. His understated contributions have been key to the Kings getting to the Stanley Cup Final in 2012.

Career Statistics		Regular Season					Playoffs				
		GP	G	A	P	Pim	GP	G	A	P	Pim
2003–04	PIT	13	1	2	3	4	DNQ				
2004–05	PIT	No Season									
2005–06	PIT	57	0	4	4	36	DNQ				
2006–07	PIT	78	1	10	11	28	5	0	0	0	2
2007–08	PIT	71	0	5	5	26	20	0	3	3	2
2008–09	PIT	81	1	15	16	18	24	1	4	5	6
2009–10	LA	73	0	11	11	21	6	0	0	0	6
2010–11	LA	82	2	13	15	16	6	0	2	2	0
2011–12	LA	82	1	8	9	16	for 2012 playoff stats see p. 18				
NHL Totals		537	6	68	74	165	61	1	9	10	16

for 2012 playoff stats see p. 18

Stoll, Jarret

b. Melville, Saskatchewan, June 25, 1982

Centre – shoots right

6'1" 215 lbs.

Drafted 36th overall by Edmonton in 2002

At 29 years of age, Stoll had been in the NHL a decade by the time the Kings went to the Stanley Cup Final in 2012. He had an outstanding junior career with Kootenay in the Western Hockey League, captaining the Ice to the Memorial Cup championship in 2001–02. That summer, Edmonton made him a second-round selection and he was assigned to Hamilton after playing a few NHL games with the Oilers.

A year later, he was with the Oilers full time and has been in the NHL ever since (with the exception of the lock-out season). Stoll had a career year in 2005–06 when he scored 22 goals and had 68 points and, not coincidentally, helped bring the team to the Stanley Cup Final. He was a mainstay with Edmonton through 2008, but that summer the Oilers couldn't resist the chance to acquire Lubomir Visnovsky from the Kings and parted with Stoll and Matt Greene in the process.

A solid two-way player, Stoll became the hero of the opening playoff round when he scored in overtime of Game 5 to eliminate Vancouver and advance the Kings one step closer to the Cup.

Career Statistics		Regular Season					Playoffs				
		GP	G	A	P	Pim	GP	G	A	P	Pim
2002–03	EDM	4	0	1	1	0					
2003–04	EDM	68	10	11	21	42					
2004–05	EDM		No Season								
2005–06	EDM	82	22	46	68	74	24	4	6	10	24
2006–07	EDM	51	13	26	39	48					
2007–08	EDM	81	14	22	36	74					
2008–09	LA	74	18	23	41	68					
2009–10	LA	73	16	31	47	40	6	1	0	1	4
2010–11	LA	82	20	23	43	42	5	0	3	3	4
2011–12	LA	78	6	15	21	60	for 2012 playoff stats see p. 18				
NHL Totals		593	119	198	317	448	35	5	9	14	32

Voynov, Slava

b. Chelyabinsk, Russia, January 15, 1990

Defence – shoots right

5'11" 202 lbs.

Drafted 32nd overall by Los Angeles in 2008

A young Russian making it in the NHL is not rare, but Slava Voynov is one of a small number of defenceman to do so. In his case, he is neither big nor imposing, but he is talented and fast.

The Kings took a chance by selecting the 18-year-old in the second round of the 2008 draft after he had played only one season in the Kontinental Hockey League. But they knew Voynov had talent as he had represented Russia at several international tournaments, notably the 2007 and 2008 U18, and three U20 tournaments – 2007, 2008, and 2009. At all five events, Voynov had won a medal – gold at his first U18, silver at his first U20 and second U18, and bronze in the other two events.

Upon being drafted, the Kings pegged him to play with Manchester in the AHL, and it was there he skated for the next three-and-a-half years. He finally earned a promotion to the Kings in early 2011–12, and he has been with the team ever since.

Career Statistics		Regular Season					Playoffs				
		GP	G	A	P	Pim	GP	G	A	P	Pim
2011-12	LA	54	8	12	20	12	for 2012 playoff stats see p. 18				
NHL Totals		54	8	12	20	12	—	—	—	—	—

Westgarth, Kevin

b. Amherstburg, Ontario, February 7, 1984

Right wing – shoots right

6'4" 243 lbs.

Undrafted

Never before has Princeton University developed a player to rival Westgarth, one of the few NHLers to have learned his skills by playing four years in the Eastern Athletic Conference.

Yet, after four seasons, he was no closer to the NHL than when he was a teenager, having been passed over in two Entry Drafts by all 30 teams. But the Kings decided to give him a shot and signed him as a free agent in March 2007 after his final game with Princeton. They assigned him to Manchester, and Westgarth continued his physical play with the Monarchs.

Westgarth played for the next three-and-a-half years in the AHL, getting into nine NHL games to whet his appetite for the real thing. The Kings deemed him to be NHL-ready at training camp in 2010, and he quickly earned his stripes by taking on several of the league's tough guys.

Despite the lack of need for such play in the post season, Westgarth still managed to get into a few games during the Kings' 2012 playoff run and, at 28, he is in the prime of his career.

Career Statistics		Regular Season					Playoffs				
		GP	G	A	P	Pim	GP	G	A	P	Pim
2008–09	LA	9	0	0	0	9	DNQ				
2009–10	LA	DNP					DNP				
2010–11	LA	56	0	3	3	105	6	0	2	2	14
2011–12	LA	25	1	1	2	39	for 2012 playoff stats see p. 18				
NHL Totals		90	1	4	5	153	6	0	2	2	14

Williams, Justin

b. Cobourg, Ontario, October 4, 1981

Right wing – shoots right

6'1" 193 lbs.

Drafted 28th overall by Philadelphia in 2000

If it sometimes feels as if half of the players with the Kings played for Philadelphia at one time, Williams only makes the case stronger. Like other Flyers' alumni Jeff Carter, Mike Richards, and Simon Gagne, Justin Williams started his pro career after being drafted into the Philly system.

He had just turned 19 by the time he played his first NHL game in 2000 after only two years of junior with Plymouth in the Ontario Hockey League, but Williams proved he belonged almost from his first shift. His skill and determination were never in question, but injuries did slow his career. He broke his hand and tore an ACL, had surgery on his shoulder and missed months recovering, but he has always bounced back.

Midway through the 2003–04 season, the Hurricanes acquired him for Danny Markov. The team missed the playoffs so Williams went overseas and played for Canada at the World Championship, winning a gold medal. He played in the Swedish Elite League during the lockout, and in his first year back the Hurricanes won the Stanley Cup.

These were his two finest years, he scored 31 and 33 goals respectively, but soon after the injuries started again. This time it was a serious knee injury and a torn Achilles tendon in consecutive years, causing him to miss more than half a season in both 2007–08 and 2008–09.

The Kings, though, continued to watch him. When they had a chance to acquire him, they did. Williams responded with two healthy seasons and 22 goals each year, and in the 2012 playoffs he was one of the team's best players at both ends of the ice.

Career Statistics		Regular Season					Playoffs				
		GP	G	A	P	Pim	GP	G	A	P	Pim
2000–01	PHI	63	12	13	25	22	DNP				
2001–02	PHI	75	17	23	40	32	5	0	0	0	4
2002–03	PHI	41	8	16	24	22	12	1	5	6	8
2003–04	PHI/CAR	79	11	33	44	64	DNQ				
2004–05	CAR	No Season									
2005–06	CAR	82	31	45	76	60	25	7	11	18	34
2006–07	CAR	82	33	34	67	73	DNQ				
2007–08	CAR	37	9	21	30	43	DNQ				
2008–09	CAR/LA	44	4	10	14	17	DNQ				
2009–10	LA	49	10	19	29	39	3	0	1	1	2
2010–11	LA	73	22	35	57	59	6	3	1	4	2
2011–12	LA	82	22	37	59	44	for 2012 playoff stats see p. 18				
NHL Totals		707	179	286	465	475	51	11	18	29	50

Coach Darryl Sutter

b. Viking, Alberta, August 19, 1958

Darryl Sutter spent his entire career as a player with one team, the Chicago Blackhawks. After he retired in 1986, he decided to go into coaching, starting in the International Hockey League before moving up to the NHL, where he has been the head coach for four different teams.

Sutter had moderate success as the Hawks coach between 1992 and 1995, after which he spent six years with the San Jose Sharks. That team never went beyond the second round of the playoffs despite many fine regular season performances, and Sutter was let go in 2002.

Later that year he resurfaced with Calgary as coach and general manager. He had little success in his home province and resigned as coach to focus on his GM duties. Again, a lack of playoff success assailed his efforts, and in 2010 he resigned as GM as well.

A full year went by and Sutter seemed uninterested in getting back into hockey, content to live on the family farm in Viking, Alberta. But when current Los Angeles GM Dean Lombardi called, Sutter listened. He accepted the position of head coach of the Kings and started work on December 22, 2011. He took a middling team to a sparkling 25–13–11 record through the rest of the season, and the Kings finished eighth in the Western Conference.

The rest is history. The Kings advanced to the Stanley Cup Final by losing only two games in three rounds and were a perfect 8–0 on the road during that stretch. Sutter's magic was extraordinary, and his timing couldn't have been better.

NHL Coaching Record		Regular Season				Playoffs		
		GP	W	L	OT	GP	W	L
1992–93	CHI	84	47	25	12	4	0	4
1993–94	CHI	84	39	36	9	6	2	4
1994–95	CHI	48	24	19	5	16	9	7
1997–98	SJ	82	34	38	10	6	2	4
1998–99	SJ	82	31	33	18	6	2	4
1999–2000	SJ	82	35	30	10	12	5	7
2000–01	SJ	82	40	27	12	6	2	4
2001–02	SJ	82	44	27	8	12	7	5
2002–03	SJ	24	9	12	2	—	—	—
2002–03	CAL	46	19	18	8	DNQ		
2003–04	CAL	82	42	30	10	26	15	11
2005–06	CAL	82	46	25	11	7	3	4
2011–12	LA	49	25	13	11	for 2012 playoff stats see p. 18		
NHL Totals		909	434	333	145	115	59	56

THE YEAR OF THE
LOS ANGELES
KINGS

Acknowledgements

The author would like to thank the many people who have helped create a worthy testament to the 2012 Stanley Cup season in such a short time. First, to publisher Doug Pepper of McClelland & Stewart and to publisher Jordan Fenn of Fenn/McClelland & Stewart. To the entire editorial team at M&S, notably editors Michael Melgaard, Linda Pruessen, Heidi Waechtler, and Rachel Geertsema, as well as Janine Laporte and David Ward. To designers Rob Scanlan and Michael Gray at First Image for managing text and images in quick and orderly, not to mention attractive, fashion. To everyone at the NHL offices who helped coordinate the publication from their end. And lastly to my own team of motivators and supporters, none of whom grew a beard in anticipation of playoff success – Liz, Ian, Zac, and Emily, my mom, whose enthusiasm knows no bounds, and my wife, Jane, whose love of hockey is, well, indescribable, really.

Photo Credits

All photos are courtesy of Getty Images